CANNIBAL-LAND

LECTOR HOUSE PUBLIC DOMAIN WORKS

CANNIBAL-LAND

MARTIN JOHNSON

ISBN: 978-93-5420-531-6

Published: 1922

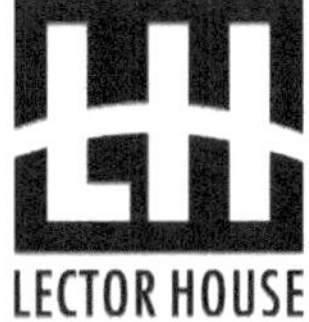

LECTOR HOUSE LLP
E-MAIL: lectorpublishing@gmail.com

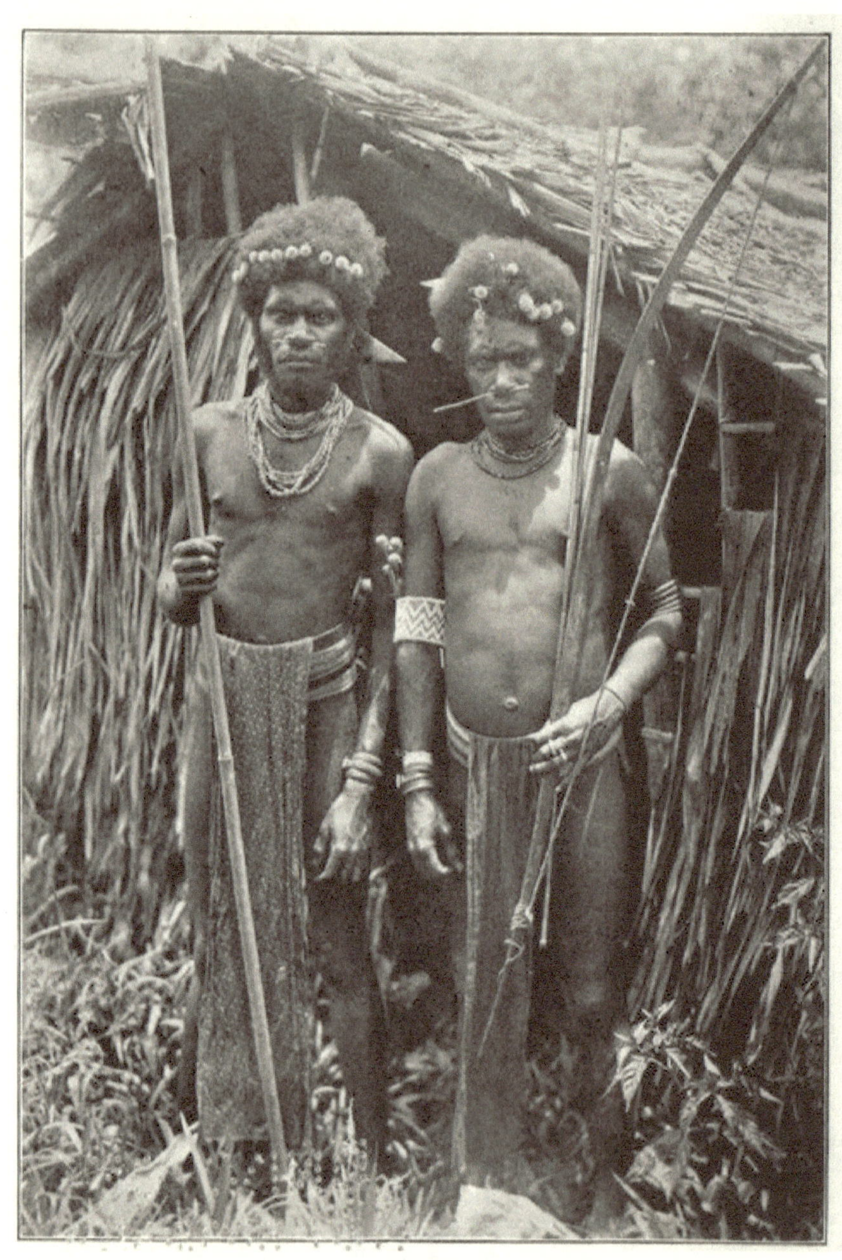

MEN OF ESPIRITU SANTO

CANNIBAL-LAND

ADVENTURES WITH A CAMERA IN THE NEW HEBRIDES

BY

MARTIN JOHNSON

WITH ILLUSTRATIONS FROM THE AUTHOR'S PHOTOGRAPHS

1922

CONTENTS

Chapter	Page
PROLOGUE	ix
I. INTRODUCING NAGAPATE	1
II. SYDNEY AND NEW CALEDONIA	10
III. THE THRESHOLD OF CANNIBAL-LAND	18
IV. NAGAPATE COMES TO CALL	23
V. IN NAGAPATE'S KINGDOM	33
VI. THE BIG NUMBERS SEE THEMSELVES ON THE SCREEN	45
VII. THE NOBLE SAVAGE	49
VIII. GOOD-BYE TO NAGAPATE	56
IX. THE MONKEY PEOPLE	59
X. THE DANCE OF THE PAINTED SAVAGES	66
XI. TOMMAN AND THE HEAD-CURING ART	74
XII. THE WHITE MAN IN THE SOUTH SEAS	79
XIII. ESPIRITU SANTO AND A CANNIBAL FEAST	85

LIST OF ILLUSTRATIONS

Page

I. MEN OF ESPIRITU SANTO iv

II. THE WATCHER OF TANEMAROU BAY 5

III. NAGAPATE 7

IV. A BEACH SCENE 11

V. LOOKING SEAWARD 16

VI. DANCE OF TETHLONG'S MEN 21

VII. A CALL FROM NAGAPATE 28

VIII. THE SAFE BEACH TRAIL, TANEMAROU BAY 31

IX. LOOKING OVER NAGAPATE'S KINGDOM FROM THE HIGH-
EST PEAK IN NORTHERN MALEKULA 35

X. WOMEN OF THE BIG NUMBERS 38

XI. RAMBI 40

XII. ATREE AND NAGAPATE 42

XIII. HUNTING FOR THE MAGIC 47

XIV. A CANNIBAL AND A KODAK 47

XV. NAGAPATE AMONG THE DEVIL-DEVILS 53

XVI. ONE OF THE MONKEY MEN 61

XVII. WO-BANG-AN-AR 64

XVIII. SOUTHWEST BAY 67

XIX. WOMAN AND CHILD OF THE LONG-HEADS, TOMMAN 69

XX. THE PAINTED DANCERS OF SOUTHWEST BAY 72

XXI. THE OLD HEAD-CURER 75

XXII. A CLUB-HOUSE IN TOMMAN WITH MUMMIED HEADS AND BODIES 78

XXIII. TOMMAN WOMEN, SHOWING GAP IN TEETH 80

XXIV. DWARFS OF ESPIRITU SANTO 88

XXV. THE CANNIBAL DANCE 91

CANNIBAL-LAND

PROLOGUE

Twelve years ago, from the deck of the Snark, I had my first glimpse of the New Hebrides.

I was standing my trick at the wheel. Jack London and his wife, Charmian, were beside me. It was just dawn. Slowly, out of the morning mists, an island took shape. The little ship rose and sank on the Pacific swell. The salt breeze ruffled my hair. I played my trick calmly and in silence, but my heart beat fast at the sight of that bit of land coming up like magic out of the gray water.

For I knew that of all the groups in the South Seas, the New Hebrides were held to be the wildest. They were inhabited by the fiercest of cannibals. On many of the islands, white men had scarcely trod. Vast, unknown areas remained to be explored. I thrilled at the thought of facing danger in the haunts of savage men.

I was young then. But my longing for adventure in primitive lands has never left me. News of a wild country, of unvisited tribes, still thrills me and makes me restless to be off in some old South Seas schooner, seeing life as it was lived in Europe in the Stone Age and is still lived in out-of-the-way corners of the earth that civilization has overlooked.

I have been luckier than most men. For my lifework has made my youthful dreams come true.

On my first voyage, in the Snark, I met with a couple of pioneer motion-picture men, who were packing up the South Seas in films to take back to Europe and America. They inspired in me the idea of making a picture-record of the primitive, fast-dying black and brown peoples that linger in remote spots. Into my boyish love of adventure there crept a purpose that has kept me wandering and will keep me wandering until I die.

Two years ago, I again found myself in the New Hebrides at dawn. London had taken the last long voyage alone; and the little Snark, so white and pretty when we had sailed it south, hung sluggishly at anchor in Api, black and stained, and wet and slimy under the bare feet of a crew of blacks. My boat now was a twenty-eight-foot open whaleboat, with a jury rig of jib and mainsail; my crew of five, squatting in the waist, looking silently at us or casting glances, sometimes down at the water, sometimes with sudden jerks of the head upward at the little mast, like monkeys under a coconut tree, were naked savages from Vao; and my companion, seated on the thwart beside me, was my wife, Osa. We were nearing the cannibal island of Malekula.

But to start the story of our adventures in Malekula at the beginning, I must go back and describe the reconnoitering trip we took fourteen months earlier.

CHAPTER I

INTRODUCING NAGAPATE

Osa and I were nearing the end of a long cruise through the South Seas. We had come in contact with many wild peoples, but none of them were quite wild enough. I had made motion-pictures of cannibals in the Solomons. They were *bona-fide* cannibals, fierce and naked. But somehow, I never quite felt that they were the real thing: they so obviously respected the English Government officers and native police boys who accompanied and protected us. I wanted to get among savages who were unspoiled—to make photographs showing them in their own villages, engaged in their ordinary pursuits. I felt sure, from what I had seen and heard and read, that the pictures I wanted were waiting to be taken in the New Hebrides and nowhere else.

Savagery has been pretty well eliminated from the South Seas. The Solomon Islander is well on the road to becoming a respectable citizen of the British Empire. Most of the Fiji Islanders have left off cannibalism and have settled down and turned Methodist. If you except New Guinea and Borneo, the New Hebrides are probably the only islands in the Pacific where there are natives who live as they did before the white man's coming.

The savages of the New Hebrides probably owe their immunity from civilization to an accident of government. For many years the ownership of the islands was disputed. Both British and French laid claim to them. Neither would relinquish hold; so finally, they arranged to administer the islands jointly until a settlement should be made. That settlement has been pending for years. Meanwhile, both governments have been marking time. Each party is slow to take action for fear of infringing on the rights—or of working for the benefit—of the other. Each maintains but a small armed force. The entire protection of the group consists of about sixty or seventy police boys, backed up by the gunboats which make occasional tours of the group. It is easy to understand that this is not an adequate civilizing force for a part of the world where civilizing is generally done at the point of a rifle, and that the savages of the more inaccessible parts of the group are as unsubdued as they were in the days of the early explorers.

I had heard that there were parts of the island of Malekula, the second largest island of the group, that no white man had ever trod, so I decided that Malekula was the island I wanted to visit. "The Pacific Islands Pilot," which I had among my books, gave a solemn warning against the people of Malekula that served only to whet my interest:

"Although an appearance of friendly confidence will often tend to allay their natural feeling of distrust, strangers would do well to maintain a constant watchfulness and use every precaution against being taken by surprise." So said the "Pilot." "... They are a wild, savage race and have the reputation of being treacherous.... Cannibalism is still occasionally practiced. Nearly all are armed with Snyders. The bushmen live entirely among the hills in small villages and are seldom seen. Being practically secure from punishment, they have not the same reasons for good behavior that the salt-water men have, and should, therefore, be always treated with caution."

A recruiter who had been for years in the New Hebrides enlisting blacks for service in the Solomons described Malekula to me in detail. It was a large island, as my map showed me, shaped roughly like an hour-glass, about sixty miles long and about ten miles across in the middle and thirty-five or so at the ends. He said that there were supposed to be about forty thousand savages on the island, most of them hidden away in the bush. The northern part of the island was shared between the Big Numbers and the Small Numbers people, who took their names from the *nambas*, the garment—if it could be called a garment—worn by the men. In the case of the Small Numbers, said my informant, it was a twisted leaf. In the case of the Big Numbers, it was a bunch of dried pandanus fiber. The recruiter said that the central part of the island was supposed to be inhabited by a race of nomads, though he himself had never seen any one who had come in contact with them. In the southern region lived a long-headed people, with skulls curiously deformed by binding in infancy.

Of all these peoples the Big Numbers were said to be the fiercest. Both British and French had undertaken "armed administrations" in their territory, in an attempt to pacify them, but had succeeded only in sacrificing a man for every savage, they had killed. No white man had ever established himself upon the territory of the Big Numbers and none had ever crossed it. I decided to attempt the crossing myself and to record the feat with my cameras.

Every one to whom I mentioned this project advised me against it. I was warned that experienced recruiters of labor for the white man's sugar and rubber plantations, who knew the islands and the natives well, never landed upon the beach unless they had a second, "covering" boat with an armed crew to protect them against treachery, and that the most daring trader planned to stop there only for a day—though perforce he often stayed for all eternity. But I had the courage born of ignorance, and ventured boldly, taking it for granted that the tales told of the savages were wildly exaggerated. Traders, missionaries, and Government officials all joined in solemn warning against the undertaking, but as none of them had ever seen a cannibal in action, I did not take their advice seriously. When they found that I was determined in my course, they gave me all the assistance in their power.

My recruiter friend suggested that I make my headquarters on Vao, a small island about a mile off the northeastern coast of Malekula, where a mission station was maintained by the French fathers. He said that between the mission and the British gunboat, which stopped there regularly, the natives of Vao had become fairly peaceable, we would be safe there, and at the same time would be in easy reach of Malekula.

Osa and I lost no time in getting to Vao, where Father Prin, an aged priest, welcomed us cordially, and set aside for us one of the three rooms in his little stone house. Father Prin had kind, beautiful eyes and a venerable beard. He looked like a saint, in his black cassock, and when we had a chance to look about at the degenerate creatures among whom he lived, we thought that he must, indeed, be one. He had spent twenty-nine years in the South Seas. During the greater part of that time he had worked among the four hundred savages of Vao. The net result of his activities was a clearing, in which were a stone church and the stone parsonage and the thatched huts of seventeen converts. The converts themselves did not count for much, even in Father Prin's eyes. He had learned that the task of bringing the New Hebridean native out of savagery was well-nigh hopeless. He knew that, once he had left his little flock, it would undoubtedly lapse into heathenism. The faith and perseverance he showed was a marvel to me. I shall always respect him and the other missionaries who work among the natives of Vao and Malekula for the grit they show in a losing fight. I have never seen a native Christian on either of the islands—and I've never met any one who has seen one!

When he learned that we were bent on visiting Malekula, Father Prin added his word of warning to the many that I had received. Though he could speak many native languages, his English was limited to *bêche-de-mer*, the pidgin English of the South Seas. In this grotesque tongue, which consorted so strangely with his venerable appearance, he told us that we would never trust ourselves among the natives if we had any real understanding of their cruelty. He said he was convinced that cannibalism was practiced right on Vao, though the natives, for fear of the British gunboat, were careful not to be discovered. He cited hair-raising incidents of poisonings and mutilations. He told us to look around among the savages of Vao. We would discover very few if any old folk, for the natives had the cruel custom of burying the aged alive. He had done everything he could to eradicate this custom, but to no end. He told us of one old woman whom he had exhumed three times, but who had finally, in spite of his efforts, met a cruel death by suffocation. Once, he had succeeded in rescuing an old man from death by the simple expedient of carrying him off and putting him into a hut next to his own house, where he could feed him and look after him. A few days after the old man had been installed, a body of natives came to the clearing and asked permission to examine him. They looked at his teeth to see if he had grown valuable tusks; they fingered his rough, withered skin; they felt his skinny limbs; they lifted his frail, helpless carcass in their arms; and finally they burst into yells of laughter. They said the missionary had been fooled—there was not a thing about the old man worth saving! We could not look for mercy or consideration from such men as these, said Father Prin. But despite his warning, Osa and I sailed away to visit the grim island.

With the assistance of Father Prin, we secured a twenty-eight-foot whaleboat that belonged to a trader who made his headquarters on Vao, but was now absent on a recruiting trip, leaving his "store" in charge of his native wife. With the aid of five Vao boys, recommended by Father Prin as being probably trustworthy, we hoisted a small jib and a mainsail, scarcely larger, and were off.

At the last moment, Father Prin's grave face awoke misgivings in me and I tried to dissuade Osa from accompanying me. Father Prin sensed the drift of our conversation and made his final plea.

"Better you stop along Vao," he urged. "Bush too bad." His eyes were anxious. But Osa was not to be dissuaded. "If you go, I'm going, too," she said, turning to me, and that was final.

We landed at a point on the Vao side of Malekula, where there were one or two salt-water villages, whose inhabitants had learned to respect gunboats. We picked up three boys to serve as guides and carriers and then sailed on to Tanemarou Bay, in the Big Numbers territory. The shores along which we traveled were rocky. Occasionally we saw a group of natives on the beach, but they disappeared as we approached. These were no salt-water savages, but fierce bushmen. Their appearance was not reassuring; but when we reached Tanemarou Bay, we boldly went ashore. We were greeted by a solitary savage who stepped out of the darkness of the jungle into the glaring brightness of the beach. He was a frightful object to behold, black and dirty, with heavy, lumpy muscles, and an outstanding shock of greasy hair. Except for a clout of dried pandanus fiber, a gorget of pig's teeth, and the pigtails that dangled from his ear-lobes, he was entirely naked. As he approached, we saw that his dull, shifty eyes were liquid; his hairy, deeply seamed face was contorted frightfully; and his hands were pressed tight against his stomach. Osa shrank close to me. But the first words of the native, uttered in almost unintelligible *bêche-de-mer*, were pacific enough. "My word! Master! Belly belong me walk about too much!"

The nervous tension that Osa and I had both felt snapped, and we burst out laughing. I saw a chance to make a friend, so I fished out a handful of cascara tablets and carefully explained to the native the exact properties of the medicine. I made it perfectly clear—so I thought—that part of the tablets were to be taken at dawn and part at sunset. He listened with painful attention, but the moment I stopped speaking he lifted the whole handful of pills to his slobbering lips and downed them at a gulp!

By this time we were surrounded by a group of savages, each as terrible-looking as our first visitor. As they made no effort to molest us, however, we gained confidence. I set up a camera and ground out several hundred feet of film. They had never seen a motion-picture camera before, but, as is often the way with savages, after a first casual inspection, they showed a real, or pretended, indifference to what they could not understand.

Through the talented sufferer who knew *bêche-de-mer*, I learned that the chief of the tribe, Nagapate, was a short distance away in the bush, and on the spur of the moment, never thinking of danger, I made up my mind to see him. Guided by a small boy, Osa and I plunged into the dark jungle, followed by our three carriers with my photographic apparatus. We slid and stumbled along a trail made treacherous by miry streams and slimy creepers and up sharp slopes covered with tough canes. At last we found ourselves in a clearing about three thousand feet above the sea.

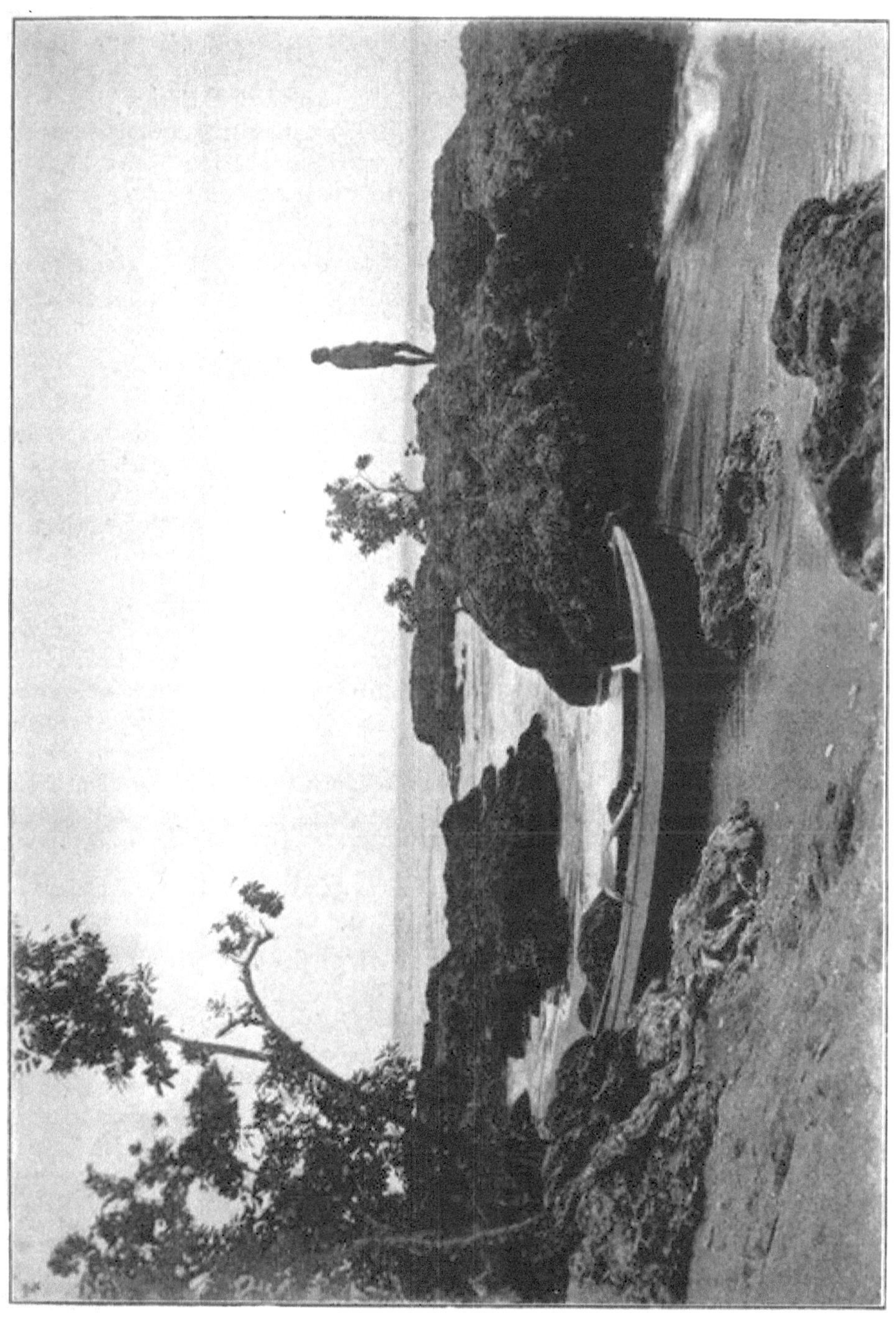

THE WATCHER OF TANEMAROU BAY

From where we stood we could see, like a little dot upon the blue of the ocean, our whaleboat hanging offshore. The scene was calm and beautiful. The brown-green slopes were silent, except for the sharp metallic calls of birds. But we knew that there were men hidden in the wild, by the faint, thin wisps of smoke that we could see here and there above the trees. Each marked a savage camp-fire. "That's where they're cooking the 'long pig,'" I said jocularly, pointing the smoke wisps out to Osa. But a moment later my remark did not seem so funny. I heard a sound and turned and saw standing in the trail four armed savages, with their guns aimed at us.

"Let's get out of this," I said to Osa; but when we attempted to go down the trail, the savages intercepted us with threatening gestures. Suddenly there burst into view the most frightful, yet finest type of savage I have ever seen. We knew without being told that this was Nagapate himself. His every gesture was chiefly.

He was enormously tall, and his powerful muscles rippled under his skin, glossy in the sunlight. He was very black; his features were large; his expression showed strong will and the cunning and brutal power of a predatory animal. A fringe of straight outstanding matted hair completely encircled his face; his skin, though glossy and healthy-looking, was creased and thick, and between his brows were two extraordinarily deep furrows. On his fingers were four gold rings that could only have come from the hands of his victims.

I thought I might win this savage to friendliness, so I got out some trade-stuff I had brought with me and presented it to him. He scarcely glanced at it. He folded his arms on his breast and stared at us speculatively. I looked around. From among the tall grasses of the clearing, there peered black and cruel faces, all watching us in silence. There were easily a hundred savages there. For the present there was no escape possible. I decided that my only course was to pretend a cool indifference, so I got out my cameras and worked as rapidly as possible, talking to the savages and to Osa as if I were completely at ease.

I soon saw, however, that we must get away if we were not to be caught by darkness. I made a last show of assurance by shaking hands in farewell with Naga-pate. Osa followed my example; but instead of releasing her, the savage chief held her firmly with one hand and ran the other over her body. He felt her cheeks and her hair and pinched and prodded her speculatively.

She was pale with fright. I would have shot the savage on the spot, but I knew that such a foolhardy act would mean instant death to both of us. I clenched my hands, forced to my lips what I hoped would pass for an amused grin, and stood pat. After a moment that seemed to both Osa and me an hour long, Nagapate released Osa and grunted an order at the savages who surrounded us. They disappeared into the bush. This was our opportunity. I ordered the three carriers to pick up the apparatus, and we started for the trail.

We had gone only a few steps when we were seized from behind. We had no chance to struggle.

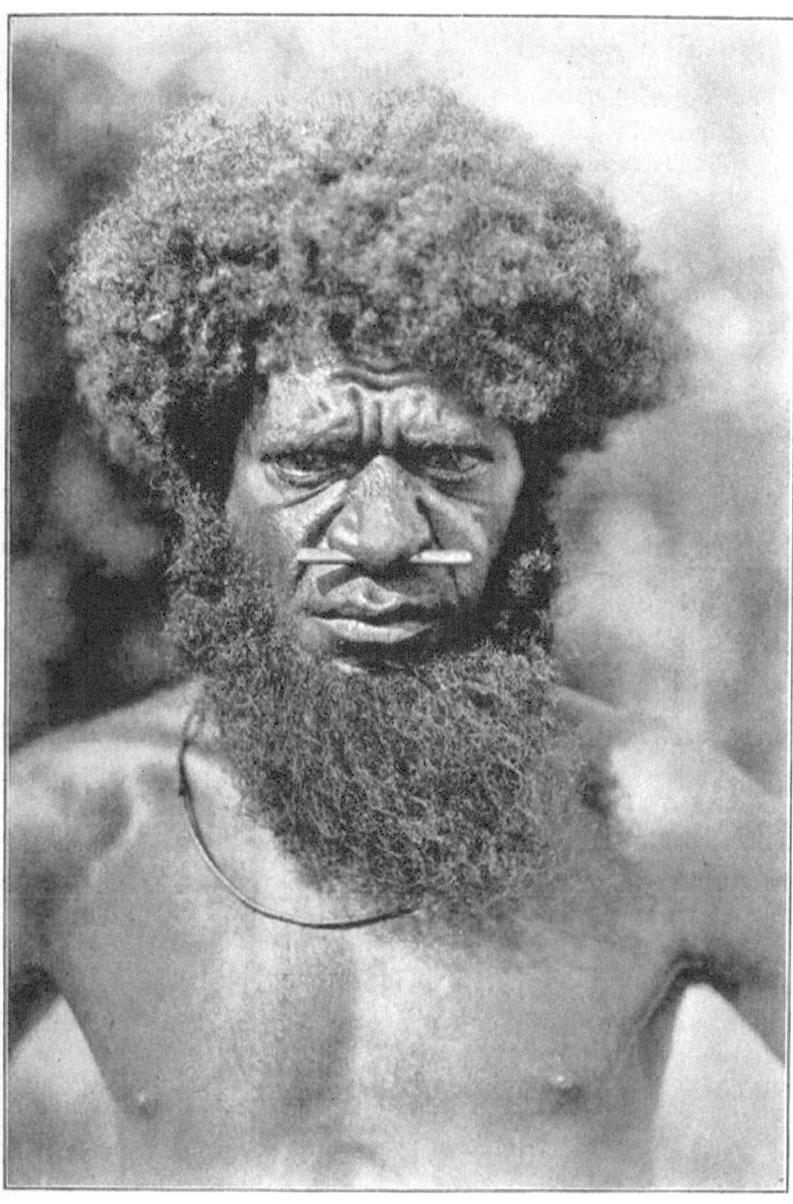

NAGAPATE

In the minutes that followed, I suffered the most terrible mental torture I have ever experienced. I saw only one slim chance for us. Osa and I each carried two revolvers in our breeches' pockets; so far, the savages had not discovered them, and I hoped there might come some opportunity to use them. Every ghastly tale I had ever heard came crowding into my memory; and as I looked at the ring of black, merciless faces, and saw my wife sagging, half-swooning, in the arms of her cannibal captors, my heart almost stopped its beating.

At this moment a miracle happened.

Into the bay far below us steamed the Euphrosyne, the British patrol-boat. It came to anchor and a ship's boat was lowered. The savages were startled. From lip to lip an English word was passed, "Man-o'-war—Man-o'-war—Man-o'-war." With an assumption of satisfaction and confidence that I did not feel, I tried to make it clear to them that this ship had come to protect us, though I knew that at any moment it might up anchor and steam away again. Nagapate grunted an order, my carriers picked up their loads, and we were permitted to start down the trail. Once out of sight we began to run. The cane-grass cut our faces, we slipped on the steep path, but still we ran.

Halfway down, we came to an open place from which we could see the bay. To our consternation, the patrol-boat was putting out to sea! We knew that the savages, too, had witnessed its departure; for at once, from hill to hill, sounded the vibrant roar of the conch-shell boo-boos—a message to the savages on the beach to intercept us.

The sun was near setting. We hurried forward; soon we found that we had lost the trail. Darkness came down, and we struggled through the jungle in a nightmare of fear. Thorns tore our clothing and our flesh. We slipped and fell a hundred times. Every jungle sound filled us with terror.

But at last, after what seemed hours, we reached the beach. We stole toward the water, hopeful of escaping notice, but the savages caught sight of us. Fortunately our Vao boys, who had been lying off in the whaleboat, sighted us, too, and poled rapidly in to our assistance. We splashed into the surf and the boys dragged us into the boat, where we lay, exhausted and weak with fear.

It took us three days to get back to Vao, but that nightmare story of storm and terror does not belong here. Suffice it to say that we at last got back safely and with my film unharmed.

On my return to Vao, one of the native boatmen presented me with a letter, which had been left for me at Tanemarou Bay, by the commander of the patrol-boat, who had been assured by our boys that we were in the immediate vicinity of the beach and were about to return to the boat.

MATANAVOT, 10th November, 1917

DEAR SIR:

I have been endeavoring to find you with a view to warning you against carrying out what I understand to be your intentions. I am told that you have decided to penetrate into the interior of this island with a view to coming in contact with the people known as the "Big Numbers." Such a proceeding cannot but be attended with great risk to yourself and all those who accompany you. The whole interior of this island of Malekula is, and has been for a considerable time, in a very disturbed condition, and it has been necessary in consequence to make two armed demonstrations in the "Big Numbers" country during the last three years. For these reasons, on the part of the Joint Administration of this group, I request that you will not proceed further with this idea, and hereby formally warn you against such persistence, for the consequences of which the Administration cannot hold itself responsible.

Yours faithfully
(Signed) M. KING
H.B.M. Resident Commissioner for the New Hebrides

In any case I trust you will not take your wife into the danger zone with you.

M. K.

CHAPTER II
SYDNEY AND NEW CALEDONIA

Osa and I were sure, after our first adventure in Malekula, that we had had enough of cannibals to last us for the rest of our natural lives. But when we reached Sydney, on our way home, and had our films developed, we began to weaken. Our pictures were so good that we almost forgot the risk we had taken to get them. The few feet I had managed to grind out on Malekula were no "staged" pictures of savage life. They were so real and convincing that Osa declared her knees went wobbly every time she saw them.

Before many months, Nagapate was scowling out of the screen at audiences in New York and Paris and London, and villagers who would never go a hundred miles from home were meeting him face to face in the Malekula jungle. The public wanted more—and so did we. Early in 1919, about a year after our first adventure in the Malekula bush, we were again in Sydney, preparing for a second visit to the land of the Big Numbers—the trip out of which this book has grown.

As we sailed into Sydney harbor on the S.S. Ventura, we met, sailing out, the Pacifique, the little steamer of the Messageries Maritimes that had taken us to the New Hebrides on our former visit. That meant we should have four weeks to wait before embarking on our journey to Malekula. We were impatient to be off, but we knew that the four weeks would pass quickly enough, for many things remained to be done before we should be ready for a long sojourn in the jungle.

We took up our abode with the Higginses, in their house on Darling Point Road overlooking the harbor. Ernie Higgins had handled my films for me on my previous trip, and I had found him to be the best laboratory man I had ever met with, so I was glad to be again associated with him.

The house was an old-fashioned brick house of about twelve or fourteen rooms. I fitted up one of the second-story rooms to serve as a workroom. I had electricity brought in and set up my Pathéscope projector, so that I could see the pictures I happened to be working on. Having this projector meant that the work of cutting and assembling films would be cut in two. I put up my rewinds, and soon had everything in apple-pie order.

From the window of my workroom, I could look over Sydney harbor. Osa and I never tired of watching the ships going in and out. We would consult the sailing lists in the newspapers, and try to identify the vessels that we saw below us. There were steamers from China and Japan and the Straits Settlements; little vessels from the various South Seas groups; big, full-rigged ships from America;

steamers from Africa and Europe; little schooners from the islands; coastal boats to and from New Zealand and Tasmania, and almost every day big ships came in with returned soldiers. In the course of a week we saw boats of every description flying the flags of almost every nation on the globe.

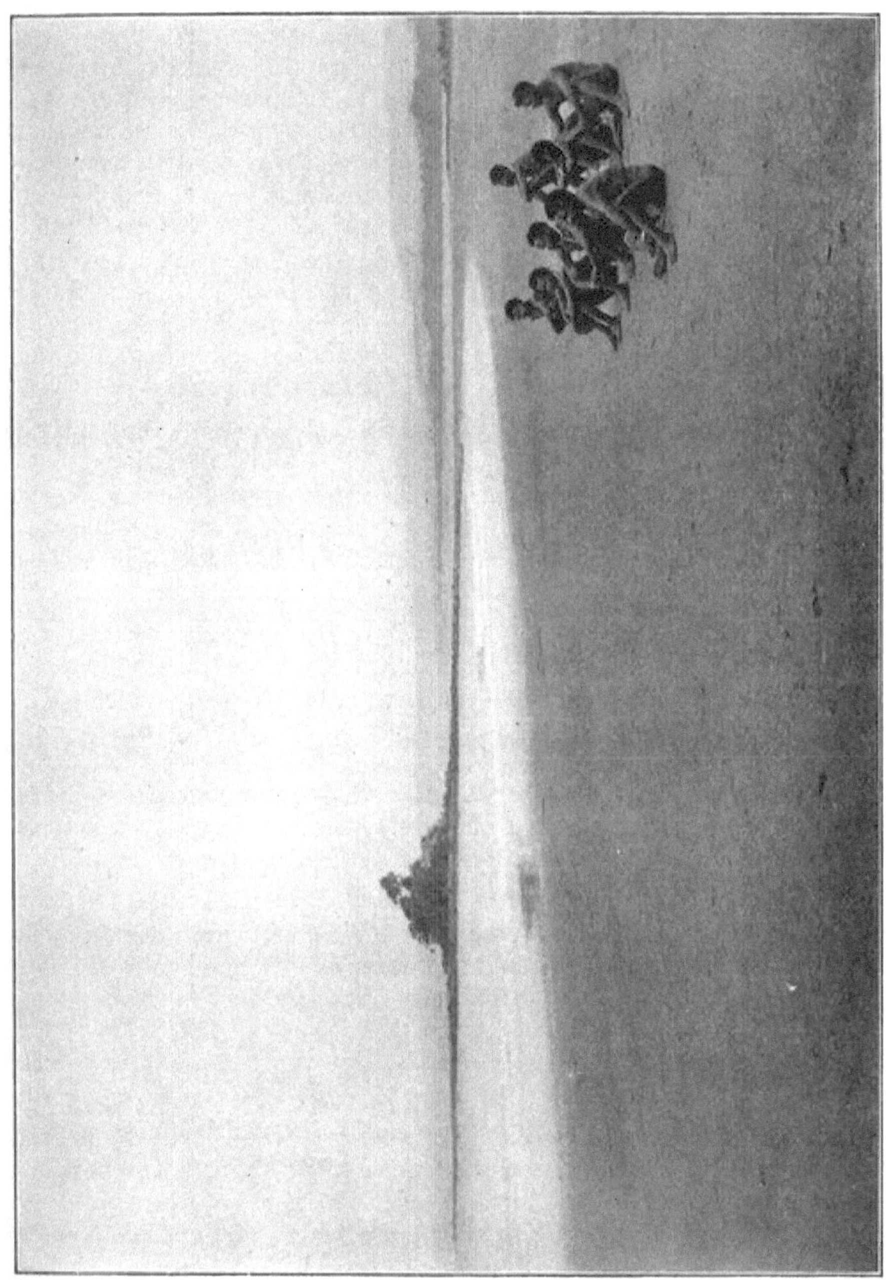

A BEACH SCENE

Osa put in long days in the harbor, fishing from Mr. Higgins's little one-man dinghy, that was nearly swamped a dozen times a day in the wash from the ferry-boats, while I worked like a slave at my motion-picture apparatus. The public thinks that a wandering camera-man's difficulties begin with putting a roll of film in the camera and end with taking it out. If I were telling the true story of this trip, I should start with my grilling weeks of preparation in New York. But my troubles in Sydney will perhaps give sufficient idea of the unromantic back-of-the-scenes in the life of a motion-picture explorer. I had troubles by the score. My cameras acted up. They scratched the film; they buckled. When I had remedied these and a dozen other ailments, I found that my pictures were not steady when they were projected. The fault we at last located in Mr. Higgins's printer. We repaired the printer. Then we found that the developer produced a granulated effect on the film. It took us two weeks to get the proper developer. But our troubles were not over. Great spots came out on the pictures—grease in the developing tanks. And the racks were so full of old chemicals that they spoiled the film that hung over them. I had new racks and new tanks made. They were not made according to specifications. I had them remade twice and then took them apart and did the work myself.

After I thought that my troubles were over, I found that my Pathéscope projector, which had been made for standard film, had several parts lacking. This was most serious, for it spoiled a plan that I had had in the back of my head ever since I had first seen my Malekula pictures. I wanted to show them to Nagapate and his men. It was an event that I had looked forward to ever since I had decided to revisit the island. It would be almost comparable to setting up a movie show in the Garden of Eden. Luckily, I was able to have the missing parts made in Sydney, and my apparatus was at last in order.

Then I had to collect as much information as I could about the New Hebrides and their inhabitants, so I trotted around morning after morning, to interview traders and steamship officials and missionaries. Another task, in which Osa helped me, was to ransack the second-hand clothing stores for old hats and coats and vests to serve as presents for the natives. Other trade-stuffs, such as tobacco, mirrors, knives, hatchets, and bright-colored calico, I planned to get in Vila, the principal port and capital of the New Hebrides.

The four weeks had gone by like a flash, but the Pacifique had not yet put in an appearance. She came limping into harbor at the end of another week. She had been delayed by engine trouble and by quarantines; for the influenza was raging through the South Seas. It was announced that she would sail in five days, but the sailing date was postponed several times, and it was the 18th of June before we finally lifted anchor.

It seemed good to get out of the flu-infested city, where theaters and schools and churches were closed, every one was forced to wear a mask, and the population was in a blue funk. We both loved Sydney and its hospitable people, but we were not sorry to see the pretty harbor, with its green slopes dotted with red-tiled roofs, fade into the distance.

Osa and I have often said that we like the Pacifique better than any ship we have ever traveled on. It is a little steamer—only one thousand nine hundred tons. We do not have bunks to sleep in, but comfortable beds. Morning coffee is served from five to eleven o'clock. It is an informal meal. Every one comes up for it in pajamas. Breakfast is at half-past eleven. Dinner is ready at half-past six and lasts until half-past eight. It is a leisurely meal, of course after course, with red wine flowing plentifully. After dinner, the French officers play on the piano and sing.

Most of the officers were strangers to us on this voyage, for our old friends were all down with the flu in Sydney. The doctor and the wireless operator were both missing, and the captain, Eric de Catalano, assumed their duties. He was a good wireless operator, for we got news from New Zealand each night and were in communication with Nouméa long before we sighted New Caledonia. How efficient he was as a doctor, I cannot say. But he had a big medicine chest and made his round each day among the sick, and though many of the passengers came down with influenza, none of them died. He was a handsome man, quiet and intelligent, and a fine photographer. He had several cameras and a well-fitted dark room and an enlarging apparatus aboard, and had made some of the best island pictures I had ever seen. He seemed to be a man of many talents, for the chief engineer told me that he had an electrician's papers and could run the engines as well as he himself could.

We were a polyglot crowd aboard. We had fifteen first-class and five second-class passengers, French, Australian, English, Scotch, and Irish, and one Dane, with Osa and myself to represent America. In the steerage were twenty-five Japanese, and up forward there was a Senegalese negro being taken to the French convict settlement at Nouméa. Our officers were all French—few could speak English. Our deck crew was composed of *libérés*—ex-convicts from Nouméa. The cargo-handlers were native New Caledonians with a sprinkling of Loyalty Islanders. The firemen were Arabs, the dish-washers in the galley, New Hebrideans. The bath steward was a Fiji Islander, the cabin steward a Hindu, the second-class cabin steward hailed from the Molucca Islands, and our table steward was a native of French Indo-China.

Three days out from Sydney we passed Middleton Reef, a coral atoll, about five miles long and two across, with the ocean breaking in foam on its reef and the water of its lagoon as quiet as a millpond. The atoll is barely above water, and many ships have gone aground there. We sailed so close that I could have thrown a stone ashore, and saw the hull of a big schooner on the reef.

As we stood by the rail looking at her, one of our fellow-passengers, a trader who knew the islands well, came up to us and told us her story.

"She went ashore three years ago, in a big wind," he said. "All hands stuck to the ship until she broke in two. Then they managed to reach land—captain and crew and the captain's wife and two children. They had some fresh water and a little food. They rationed the water carefully, and there was rain. But the food soon gave out. For days they had nothing. The crew went crazy with hunger, and killed one of the children and ate it. For two days, the mother held the other child in her arms. Then she threw it into the sea so that they could not eat it. Then three of the men took one of the ship's boats. They could not manage it in the rough sea, but by a lucky chance they were washed up on the beach. They were still alive, but the captain's wife had lost her mind."

We reached Nouméa on the morning of June 23d. The pilot met us outside the reef, in accordance with regulations, but he refused to come on board when he found that we had several passengers down with the influenza, so we towed him in. We were not allowed to land, but were placed in quarantine off a small island about two miles from Nouméa, between the leper settlement and Île Nou, the convict island. We were avoided as though we had leprosy. Each day a launch came with fresh meat and fresh vegetables, the French engineer and black crew all masked and plainly anxious not to linger in our vicinity any longer than necessary, and each day the doctor came and took our temperatures.

We passed our time in fishing from the deck. We had excellent luck and our catches made fine eating. Osa, of course, caught more fish than any one else, principally because she was up at sunrise and did not quit until it was time to go to bed. I relieved the monotony in the evenings by showing my pictures. I set up the Pathéscope in the saloon, and each night I gave a performance. My audience was most critical. Every one on board knew the New Hebrides and Nouméa well, and many of the passengers were familiar with the Solomons and other groups in which I had taken pictures. But my projector worked finely; I had as good a show as could be seen in any motion-picture house, and every one was satisfied.

We had been surprised, as we steamed into the harbor, to see the Euphrosyne lying at anchor there. The sight of her had made us realize that we were indeed nearing the Big Numbers territory. Strangely enough, the thought aroused no fear in us—only excitement and eagerness to get to work, and resentment against the delay that kept us inactive in Nouméa harbor.

Not until four days had passed was our quarantine lifted. On the evening of June 27th, the launch brought word that peace had been signed, and that, if no more cases of flu had developed, we would be allowed to land on the following day and take part in the peace celebration.

New Caledonia does not much resemble the other islands of the South Pacific. It has a white population of twenty thousand—about two thirds as great as the native population. Its capital, Nouméa, is an industrial city of fifteen thousand white inhabitants—the Chicago of the South Seas. In and around it are nickel-smelters, meat-canneries, sugar-works, tobacco and coconut-oil and soap factories. New Caledonia is rich in minerals. It has large deposits of coal and kaolin, chrome and cobalt, lead and antimony, mercury, cinnabar, silver, gold and copper and gypsum and marble. In neighboring islands are rich guano beds. Agriculture has not yet been crowded off the island by industry. The mountain slopes make good grazing grounds and the fertile valleys are admirably fitted for the production of coffee, cotton, maize, tobacco, copra, rubber, and cereals. Yet there is little of South Seas romance about the islands. And Nouméa is one of the ugliest, most depressing little towns on the face of the earth.

We docked there early on the morning of Saturday, the 28th of June. The wharf was packed with people, but none of them would come on board. We might have been a plague ship. As we went ashore, we looked for signs of the peace celebration. A few half-hearted firecrackers and some flags hanging limp in the heat were all. The real celebration, we were told, would take place on Monday.

In the evening, we were invited to attend one of those terrible home-talent performances that I had thought were a product only of Kansas, but, I now learned, were as deadly in the South Seas as in the Middle West. A round little Frenchman read a paper in rapid French that we could not understand, but the expression of polite interest on the faces of the audience told us that it must be like the Fourth-of-July orations in our home town. Then came a duet, by a man and woman who could not sing. Another paper. Then an orchestra of three men and four girls arranged themselves with much scraping of chairs on the funny little stage and wheezed a few ancient tunes.

On Sunday night we went to the Peace Ball in the town hall. Most of Nouméa's fifteen thousand inhabitants were there, so dancing was next to impossible. It was like a Mack Sennet comedy ball. Ancient finery had been hauled out for the occasion, and, though most of the men appeared in full dress, scarcely one had evening clothes that really fitted. Under the too loose and too tight coats, however, there were warm and hospitable hearts, and we were treated royally. After the ball, we were entertained at supper by the governor and his suite.

Governor Joulia was a little, bald-headed man of about fifty years of age, always smiling, always polite, and always dressed in the most brilliant of brilliant uniforms, covered with decorations that he had won during campaigns in Senegal, Algeria and India. His wife was a pretty, plump woman of about thirty—she and Osa took to each other at once. They spoke no English, and our French is awful, but we struck out like drowning persons, and managed to understand each other after a fashion.

On Monday, the "real celebration" of the peace consisted in closing the stores and sleeping most of the day. In the afternoon, the governor and his wife came to the ship for us and took us to their beautiful summer place, about five miles from the city. A great park, with deer feeding under the trees, fine gardens, tennis courts, well-tended walks—and the work all done by numbered convicts.

There are convicts everywhere in and about Nouméa—convicts and *libérés*. Their presence makes the ugly little town seem even more unprepossessing than it is. The pleasantest spot anywhere around is Île Nou, the convict island that I have often heard called a hell on earth. On this green little island are about five hundred convicts—all old men, for France has not deported any of her criminals to New Caledonia since 1897. They are all "lifers." Indeed, I was told of one old man who is in for two hundred years; he has tried to escape many times, and, according to a rule of the settlement, ten years are added to a man's sentence for each attempt at escape.

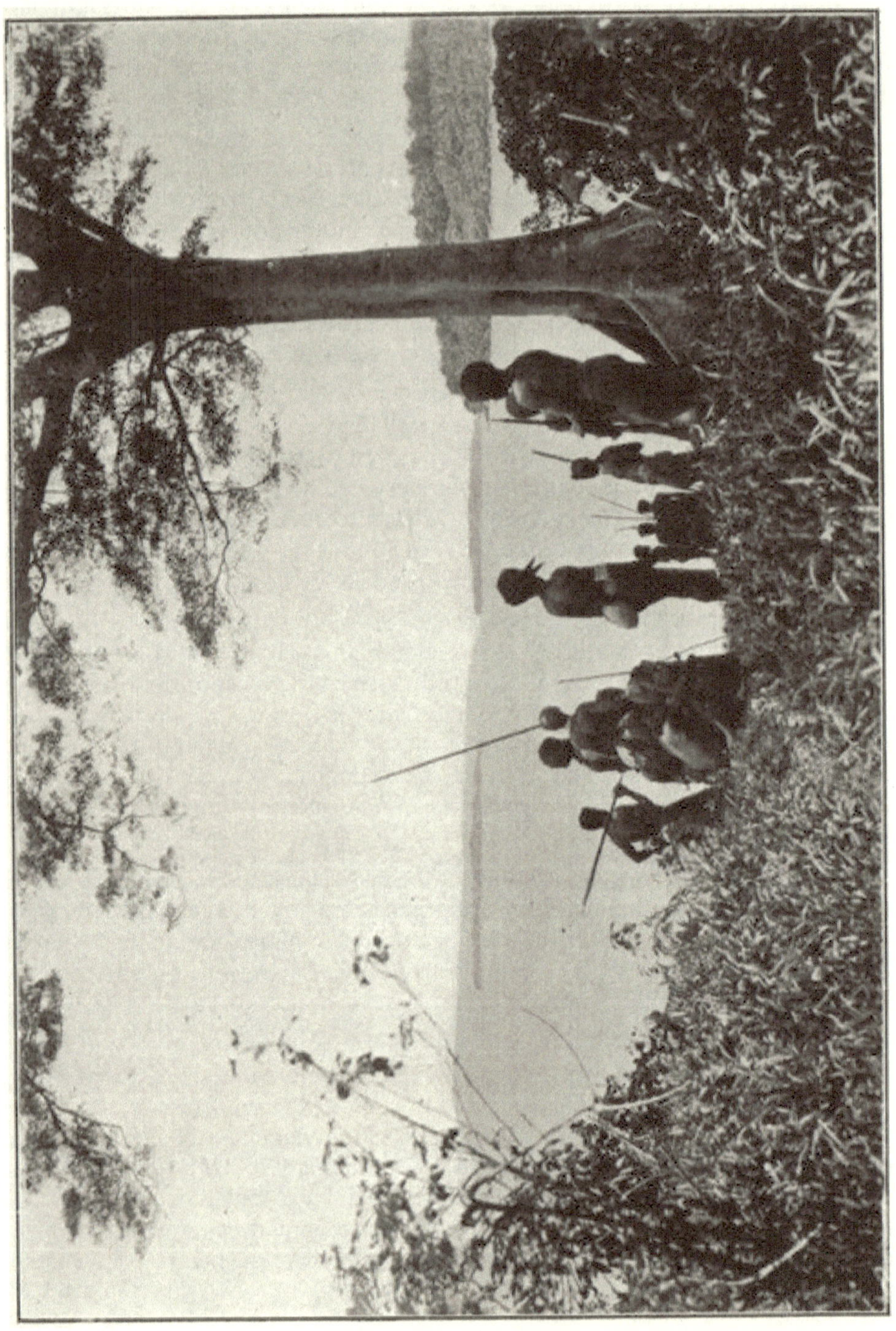

LOOKING SEAWARD

We visited Île Nou in company with Governor Joulia and Madame Joulia; the Mayor of Nouméa; the manager of the big nickel mines; the Governor of the prison settlement, and a lot of aides-de-something. We saw the old prisoners, in big straw hats and burlap clothing, each with his number stamped on his back, all busy doing nothing. We were taken through the cells where, in former times, convicts slept on bare boards, with their feet through leg-irons. We were locked in dark dungeons, and, for the benefit of my camera, the guillotine was brought out and, with a banana stalk to take the place of a man, the beheading ceremony was gone through with. We were taken in carriages over the green hills to the hospitals and to the insane asylum, where we saw poor old crazy men, with vacant eyes, staring at the ceilings. Here we met the king of the world, who received us with great pomp from behind the bars of a strong iron cage, and a pitiful old inventor, who showed us a perpetual-motion machine which he had just perfected. It was made from stale bread.

Yet Île Nou is better than Nouméa, with its ugly streets full of broken old *libé-rés*. While most of the convicts were sent out for life, some were sent for five years. At the end of that time, they were freed from Île Nou and permitted to live in New Caledonia on parole, and if they had committed no fresh offense, at the end of another five years they were given their ticket back to France. Any one sentenced to a longer term than five years, however, never saw France again. He regained his freedom, but was destined to lifelong exile. Some of the *libérés* have found employ-ment and have become responsible citizens of New Caledonia, but many of them drift through the streets of Nouméa, broken old men who sleep wherever they can find a corner to crawl into and pick their food from the gutters.

I was glad, while in Nouméa, to renew my acquaintance with Commission-er King of the New Hebrides, who had come to New Caledonia to have the Eu-phrosyne repaired. I talked over with him my proposed expedition to Malekula, and received much valuable advice. He could not give me the armed escort I had hoped to secure from him, for he had no police boys to spare. He promised, how-ever, to pick us up at Vao, in about a month's time, and take us for a cruise through the group in the Euphrosyne. I wanted him, and the New Caledonian officials as well, to see some of my work, so I decided to show my films in the Grand Ciné-ma, the leading motion-picture house of Nouméa. I gave the proprietor the films free of charge, under condition that I got fifty seats blocked off in the center of the house. We invited fifty guests, and the remainder of the house was packed with French citizens of Nouméa, Chinese and Japanese coolies and native New Caledo-nians. I showed the five reels called "Cannibals of the South Seas." Then I showed my four reels of Malekula film, and ended up with a one-reel subject, Nouméa. We were given an ovation, and both Osa and I had to make speeches — understood by few of those present. The French have a passion for speeches whether they can understand them or not. The next morning, we found ourselves celebrities as we walked through the streets of Nouméa.

CHAPTER III

THE THRESHOLD OF CANNIBAL-LAND

We left New Caledonia at midnight on July 3d, and steamed over a calm sea to Vila.

Vila is the commercial center as well as the capital of the New Hebrides and its harbor is one of the finest in the South Seas. On our right, as we steamed in, was the island of Irriki, a mountain peak rising out of the sea, on the highest point of which Mr. King has built his house. Vila is a typical South Seas town—a rambling mixture of tropical and European architecture and no architecture at all. Its public buildings, French and British, its churches, and the well-kept British settlement, with the parade grounds and barracks for the native police, make it more imposing than the run of the pioneer villages of Melanesia, but it seemed strange to us that it should be the metropolis for the white people of thirty islands. We spent a day in Vila looking up old acquaintances and laying in supplies. Among the acquaintances we found good old Father Prin who had been retired from active duty on Vao and had come to Vila to spend his declining days. He was glad to see us, but shook his head when he heard that we were again going to try our luck among the Big Numbers.

"Big Numbers plenty bad," he warned us in *bêche-de-mer*. And Osa and I replied in the same tongue, "Me no fright."

I bought nearly a thousand dollars' worth of food and trade-stuffs from the four trading stores of Vila, but could not get a schooner or any native boys to take us on our trip around Malekula. So I decided to go on to the island of Espiritu Santo, two hundred miles to the north. We stopped at Api, to leave mail and supplies and to take on copra. In the harbor there, we again saw the old Snark at anchor. It was a black and shabby ship, manned by a black crew and used for recruiting labor for work in the white man's sugar and copra plantations.

We found Segond Channel, off Southeastern Santo, filled with cutters and schooners, every one of which had white men aboard, who had been waiting a couple of weeks for the news and supplies brought by the Pacifique. In no time at all, I made arrangements for three schooners with big crews to accompany me on my visit to the tribe of the Big Numbers. Mr. Thomas, of Hog Harbor, promised he would send his boat to Vao in a week with as many boys as he could spare. Mr. Perrole, an experienced French recruiter, also agreed to charter a schooner and bring boys. We obtained a third schooner from a young Frenchman, Paul Mazouyer, one of the most picturesque dare-devils I have ever met. A giant in size and strength, boiling with energy, always singing, sometimes dancing with his boys, he did not understand the meaning of fear. He was a match for three white men, and he took chances on the beach that no other recruiter would dream of taking. I asked him once in *bêche-de-mer*—the only language in which we could converse—if the savages did not sometimes make him a little anxious.

"Ah," he said, shifting his huge frame and stretching his arms, "my word! Suppose fifty men he come, me no fright!"

I believed him. He was a two-fisted adventurer of the old type, with the courage of unbeaten youth. He knew, as every white man in the New Hebrides knows, that he might expect short shrift once the natives got him in their power, but he trusted to fate and took reckless chances.

The captain of the Pacifique agreed to take us to Vao, although it was fifty miles off his course. We dropped anchor off the island just at daylight and were surrounded almost immediately by canoes filled with naked savages. The Pacifique was a marvel to the natives. She was one of the smallest steamers I had ever been aboard, but they had never in all their lives seen so large a vessel. The imposing size of the ship and the impressive quantity of my baggage—sixty-five trunks, crates and boxes—gave me a great deal of importance in their eyes. As we stood on the beach watching the unloading of the ship's boat, they crowded about, regarding us with furtive curiosity. From time to time they opened their huge, slobbering mouths in loud guffaws, though there was apparently no cause for laughter.

When my things were all unloaded, the captain and officers shook hands with us and put off for the ship. In twenty minutes the Pacifique was steaming away. Before she gained speed, a big American flag was hoisted between the masts, and the engineer tooted encouragement to us. As she grew small in the distance, the flag at the stern of the vessel was dipped three times. We sat on the beach among our boxes and watched her until she was just a cloud of smoke on the horizon. We felt very lonely and very much shut off from our kind there, surrounded by a crowd of jabbering, naked savages, who stared at us with all the curiosity shown by people back home toward the wild man in a sideshow.

With a show of cheerfulness, we set about making ourselves comfortable for the weeks to come. The huts of the seventeen converts were deserted, and rapidly going to pieces: the former occupants had forsaken the lonely clearing for the crowded villages. But the little stone house in which Father Prin had lived was still standing, though one corner of the roof had fallen in. A proffer of tobacco secured me many willing black hands to repair the roof and thatch it with palm leaves. Other natives brought up our trunks and boxes. They cut big poles and lashed the boxes to them with vines, and, ten to twenty natives to a box, they carried the luggage from the beach in no time. By noon we had everything stored away safe from the weather. We spent the afternoon in unpacking the things needed for immediate use, and soon Osa and I had our little three-room dwelling shipshape.

We had learned a lesson from our first trip, with the result that, on this second expedition, we had brought with us every possible comfort and even some luxuries—from air-cushions and mattresses to hams, bacons, and cheeses specially prepared for us in Sydney. With a clear-flamed Primus stove and Osa to operate it, we were fairly certain of good food. Having promulgated the law of the New Hebrides and Solomons, that every native coming upon the clearing must leave his gun behind him and cover his nakedness with calico, we settled down for a long stay.

Vao is a very small island, no more than two miles in diameter, lying several miles off the northeast shore of Malekula. It is rimmed on the Malekula side by a broad, beautiful beach. Three small villages are hidden in the low, scrub jungle, but the only signs of habitation are three canoe houses that jut out from the fringe of bushes and hundreds of canoes drawn up in a careful line upon the beach.

About four hundred savages live in the three villages of Vao. Their huts—mere shelters, not high enough to permit a man to stand erect—contain nothing but a few bits of wood to feed the smoldering fires. Pigs wander freely in and out. Oftentimes these animals seem to be better favored than the human inmates, who are a poor lot, many of them afflicted with dreadful sores and weak eyes.

Many of the inhabitants of Vao are refugees from the big island of Malekula, who were vanquished in battle and literally driven off the earth by their enemies. Soon after our arrival, a powerful savage named Tethlong, one of the Small Numbers people, arrived on Vao with twenty of his men. All the remaining men of his tribe had been killed and the women and children had been taken captive. The natives of Vao received the newcomers as a welcome addition to their fighting force, and Tethlong set about to insure his position among his new neighbors. He invited the entire population to a feast, and at once sent his men to neighboring islands to buy up pigs and chickens for the occasion. The devil-devils—great, hollowed logs, carved roughly to represent human faces, which are erected everywhere in the New Hebrides to guard against evil spirits—were consulted to find a propitious time for the feasting, and on the appointed day the celebration began with much shouting and singing and dancing and beating of tom-toms. It lasted for several days. Before it was over, seven hundred and twenty pigs had been slaughtered. The island had never before seen such a feast. As a result of his political strategy, Tethlong became the Big Chief of Vao, taking precedence over the chiefs already there.

I got some fine pictures of Tethlong's feast, but they were the only pictures I took for some days. For one thing, I was too busy for camera work; for the job of checking over our supplies and fortifying our place against a heavy rain kept us busy. For another, I was anxious to keep our savage neighbors at a distance, so long as we were alone.

Though they got over their curiosity concerning us and our effects within a few days, about half a dozen loafers continued to appear every morning and beg for tobacco. They were too lazy to work, and their constant presence annoyed us. They were in the way, and, besides, they grew cheekier day by day. The limit was reached one evening when Osa was playing her ukulele. Several natives wandered over from the village to listen. It was pretty music—I liked it a lot—and Osa was flattered when some of the boys came to talk to us about it. But it soon developed that they were demanding tobacco as compensation for listening!

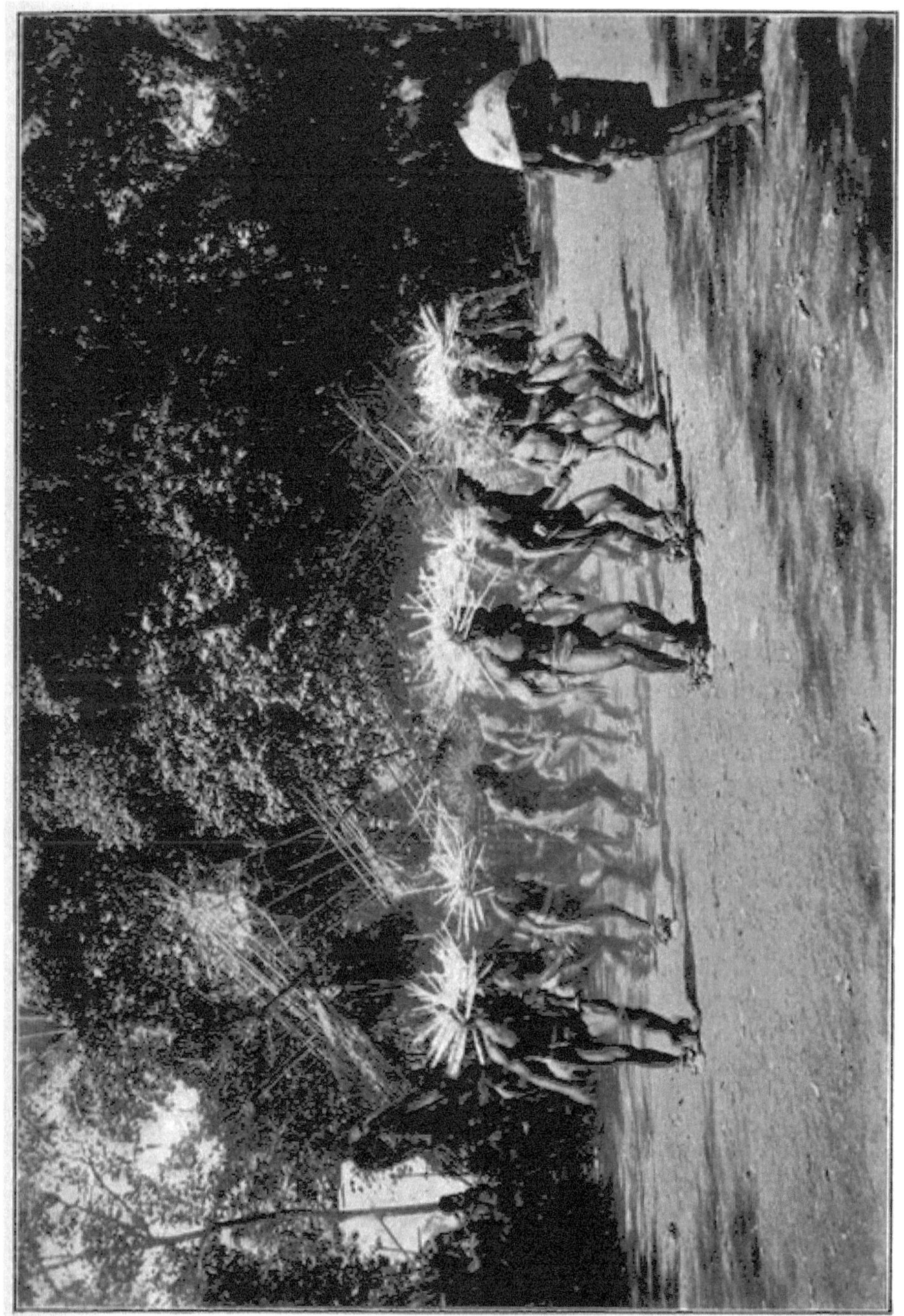

DANCE OF TETHLONG'S MEN

We managed to get hold of a fairly trustworthy boy—Arree by name—to help with the housework. He claimed to have gone to the Catholic mission school at Vila, and, strange to say, he did not approve of the ways of his own people, though he was never absent from one of their festivals. He always told us the local gossip. It was from him that we learned what had happened to the mission boy who had worked for us on our former visit. He had aroused the ill-will of a neighbor and two weeks before our arrival had died from poison placed in his *lap-lap*, a pudding made of coconuts and fish.

Osa could write volumes regarding the difficulties of training her scrubby native recruit to the duties of housework. He spoke good *bêche-de-mer*, but *bêche-de-mer* is a language capable of various interpretations. Osa spoke it better than I, but even she could not make simple orders clear to our muddle-brained black slavey. One morning, she told Arree to heat an iron for her. She waited for a long time to get it, and then went after it. She found Arree crouched before the fire, gravely watching the iron boiling in a pot.

Arree murdered the King's English in a way that must have made old Webster turn over in his grave. He never said "No." His negative was always "No more," and his affirmative was an emphatic "Yes-yes." When I called for warm water in the morning, he would reply, blandly, "Hot water, he cold fellow," and I would have to wait until, in his leisured way, Arree built the fire and heated the water. He had a sore leg, which I healed with a few applications of ointment. A few days later, he came to me with one eye swollen nearly shut, and my medicine kit in his hand. "Me gottem sore leg along eye-eye," he informed me. Sometimes he achieved triumphs. I asked him once to tell another native to bring me the saw from Osa. In order to air his knowledge of English, Arree said: "You go along Mary (woman) belong Master catchem one fellow something he brother belong ackus (axe), pullem he come, pushem he go." And then he translated the command, for his admiring, wide-eyed brother, into the native dialect.

Osa and I often caught ourselves falling into this queer English even when there were no natives around. It gets into the blood like baby-talk.

CHAPTER IV

NAGAPATE COMES TO CALL

Long before our reënforcements were due to arrive, we began to feel uneasy on Vao. I found our neighbors far too friendly with the unregenerate Malekula bushmen to be entirely trustworthy. The bush people had no canoes. But when they wanted to visit Vao, they would sing out from the shore, and the Vao men would go after them and bring them over, fifteen or twenty of them at a time. The Malekula men never came near our clearing, but the knowledge that they were on the island made us uncomfortable. We were sure that they came to participate in savage orgies, for often after a group of them arrived, the sound of the tom-tom and of savage chanting drifted through the jungle from the native villages, and our little clearing seemed haunted by shadows that assumed menacing shapes. Finally, there occurred an incident that changed what had been merely nervous apprehension to vivid fear.

We had been a week on the island. The schooners we were awaiting had not yet arrived. We could expect them, now, any day, but things do not run by clockwork in the South Seas, so we knew that another week might pass before we should see them. It had been hot and rainy and steamy and disagreeable ever since our arrival, but to-night was clear, with a refreshing breeze. After our tinned dinner, Osa and I went down to the beach. The moon was full. The waves lazily washed up on the soft sand, white in the moonlight, and the fronds of the palm-trees along the shore whispered and rattled above our heads. Osa, in a romantic mood, was strumming very softly on the ukulele. All at once, we heard the whish-whish of canoe paddles coming around a rocky point. We moved back into the shelter of some bushes and watched.

Presently ten natives landed on the beach and drew their canoe up after them. From it they took two objects wrapped in leaves, one elongated and heavy—it took several men to handle it—the other small and round. Soon the men, with their burdens, disappeared down a dark pathway leading to the village.

For several minutes we did not dare to move. Then we hurried back to the house and got our revolvers and sat for a long time feeling very much alone, afraid to go to bed and afraid to go out in the open. After a while a weird chanting and the beating of tom-toms began in the village near by. The noise kept us awake all night.

Next morning, Arree came up with his story of the night's revels. The packages, he said, had really contained the body and head of a man. The head had been impaled on a stick in the village square, and the natives had danced wildly around it. Then the body was spitted on a long pole and roasted over a great fire. The savages continued to dance and sing until the horrible meal was ready. The rest of the night was spent in feasting. Such orgies as this, Arree said, were fairly frequent. The natives often purchased slain enemies from the bush savages of Malekula, to eat as they would eat so many pigs.

Two days after this incident, Paul Mazouyer dropped anchor off Vao. We were glad to see him, and told him so in emphatic *bêche-de-mer*, the only common language at our disposal. We promptly put my apparatus aboard his little schooner, or cutter, as the craft was called in those waters, and set sail for the country of the Big Numbers. A hundred naked savages watched us in silence from the beach. The two other schooners had gone on ahead to meet us in Big Numbers Bay, known locally as Tanemarou. They were all recruiting schooners with experienced crews, armed with regulation rifles, as permitted and indeed insisted upon by the Government.

Recruiting labor for the rubber and sugar plantations of white settlers is a regular business in the New Hebrides and a dangerous one. A recruiter chooses his island and anchors in the offing. He then sets adrift a charge of dynamite, which is detonated as a signal to the natives. The roar of the explosion rolls through the valleys and echoes against the hills. On the day following, the savages come down to the beach to trade. Two boats then put off from the schooner. In the first is the white man with an unarmed crew, for the savages are not beyond rushing the boat for the sake of a gun. In the second, hovering a short distance away, is an armed crew, who cover the savages with their guns while their master parleys with the chiefs for recruits. At the first hostile move on the part of the natives, the boys in the covering boat open fire.

Despite such extreme precautions, tragedies happen. A friend of Paul Mazouyer's had been killed at Malua, whither we were now bound. Paul told us the story. There were only a few savages on the beach at the time; but one of them promised to go into the bush to recruit if his people were given half a case of tobacco. The recruiter foolishly sent his covering boat back to the cutter for the tobacco, and the savages sat down on the beach to wait. While they were waiting, another savage came out of the jungle. He walked slowly down the beach with his hands behind him and waded out into the water until he could get behind the white man. Then he suddenly placed the muzzle of a gun against the white man's back and pulled the trigger.

A French gunboat was sent from Nouméa to avenge the murder, and a month after the tragedy Paul led an expedition into the bush which razed a village and killed a number of savages.

In conclusion, Paul told us an incident that he thought was uproariously funny. The victor had brought the bodies of four of the natives down to the sea. Among the members of the expedition were a dozen "civilized" blacks of a tribe hostile to the Big Numbers. These twelve boys looked thoughtfully at the four dead bodies and then approached the commander with a spokesman at their head.

"Master," he said with great earnestness, "me lookum some fellow man he die finish. He stop along sand. He plenty good kai-kai! Me think more better you no put him along ground. Altogether boy he speak—He eat him!"

We reached the bay where these events had taken place on the first night after our departure from Vao. We coasted along so close to the shore that we could plainly see groups of natives who watched us, talking and gesticulating among themselves, and sometimes followed us for some distance along the beach, curious to see where we would land. We rounded the northern point of the island and bucked into a stiff head wind and a strong current. We made little progress until the tide turned. Then we went along at a good rate.

We anchored in Malua Bay, a stone's throw from shore, on a line with a great ravine that cleft the mountains and separated the territory of the Small Numbers tribes, which lies directly across from Vao, from that of the Big Numbers, which occupies the northwest corner of the island.

That was a night typical of the South Seas. I shall never forget it. The moon was visible for only a few seconds at a time, when it dodged from behind thick, drifting clouds and drenched everything with a light almost as bright as day. Our black crew huddled in the bow of the boat. We sat with our guns beside us. On the shore we could clearly make out the forms of savages squatting around their camp-fire. From the distance we could hear the deep tones of the conch-shell boo-boos. The sea rolled upon the beach with a heavy, sleepy purring. In the dark blue waters below us we could see sharks moving about, leaving trails of phosphorus. By the light of a greasy, smoky lantern that went out every few moments, struggling against a ground swell that threatened to capsize my typewriter, I entered the day's events in my diary. As I wrote, the savages began a weird dance, their grotesque forms silhouetted against the sky. The sound of their chanting brought me what Osa calls the "South Sea feeling." I don't know how to describe it. But it is the thing that makes me always want to go back.

The next morning we went ashore in two boats, Paul, Osa, and myself in one, with one boy to pull, and four armed boys in another boat to cover us. There were only half a dozen savages in sight, so we landed on the beach and even walked up to the small river that emptied into the bay, but we kept our guns handy and the covering boat was watching closely. We knew that if it came to a rush, we could beat the savages to the boat and that they were too poor shots to waste valuable ammunition in shooting from the edge of the jungle. It is the custom of the men of Malekula to approach near enough to place the muzzle against their enemy. Otherwise, they seldom risk a shot.

We had not been ashore long when we saw a couple of natives emerge from the bush and walk toward us. We hurried to the boat. Other savages appeared in small groups, so we shoved off. We bobbed along the shore all afternoon, while Paul tried to get recruits. About fifty armed savages wandered up and down, coaxing us in closer; but on account of Osa, I would not risk landing, though Paul, who feared nothing, wanted to put in to shore. He knew that almost any savage in that region would kill him, if chance offered, in revenge for the part he had played in the punitive expedition, but this was his favorite recruiting ground and he was not to be scared away from it. He had the contempt for natives that has resulted fatally for many a white man.

At sundown we returned to the cutter. We could hear the savages shouting as they went back into the hills. The broiling sun had left us hot and sticky, and when Paul suggested a swim we all agreed to it, sharks or no sharks. The boys kept a sharp lookout for the flashes of phosphorus that would mean approaching danger, but we finished our swim without adventure. Nevertheless, that night we put out hooks and caught two sharks, one four feet long, the other six—which ended our swimming along these shores.

Paul's little boat was close quarters for the three of us. He made his bed alongside the engines, below, and Osa and I slept in the scuppers, one on each side of the hatch.

At about eleven o'clock, it began to rain and blow. We dragged our anchor and had to put down another and then a kedge anchor in addition. The craft twisted and turned and plunged, until Osa swore we went right over and up again. I padded Osa with old sail to protect her from bruises and we held on to the hatch with both hands to keep from being thrown into the sea. Almost all our supplies were drenched; for we robbed everything else of tarpaulin or canvas coverings to keep my apparatus dry. Shivering and wretched, we crouched on deck waiting for daylight. Morning was never so slow in coming; but with the first light, the rain ceased, the sea became smooth, and the sun came up broiling hot, sucking up the moisture until from stern to bow we looked like a spout of a boiling tea-kettle.

There was fever in the air. We ate quinine as if it had been candy, in an effort to stave off the sickness that, always inconvenient, would now prove especially so.

About noon we made out two vessels sailing up to us, and as they came alongside we found that one was sailed by Perrole and the other by a young man, half Samoan and half English, whom Mr. Thomas had sent with ten boys. His name was Stephens. We now had twenty-six armed and experienced natives, four white men and Osa. With this force I was ready to undertake almost anything; so after a hasty conference we decided to go on to Tanemarou, the bay from which we had first entered Nagapate's territory. Without the aid of the Government, I saw that it would be impossible to carry out my original intention of entering the island at the northern end and traversing it straight through to the southern. So I proposed the alternative plan of sailing completely around the island, landing at different points from which I could strike inland to visit the tribes. In many ways, this latter plan proved to be the better of the two for my purpose. I doubt, now, if a Government escort would have been to my advantage; for any Government expedition would have been regarded as a punitive raid and as such would have encountered the most determined resistance. Even at the time, I felt that the peaceable nature of my expedition would put me on good terms with the savages. Cruel as they were, they were childlike, too, and the fact that we were coming to them in a friendly spirit with presents for which, apparently, we were asking nothing in return, would, I felt sure, disarm their hostility. I had discovered that most of the recent murders of white men had been committed by the savages in a spirit of revenge. Recruiters who had carried off their kinsfolk; traders who had cheated them; members of punitive expeditions, or the occasional Simon Legree who had earned the hatred of the blacks by cruelty—such were the victims of savage gun or knife.

It was with a feeling of confidence that I sailed into Tanemarou Bay. Here, sweeping around us, was the broad beach across which we had run for our lives almost two years before. In fine yellow sand it spread away from the water's edge for about a hundred yards to the dark fringe of jungle. Against the high black volcanic rocks that guarded the entrance to the bay, a heavy surf beat and roared, but on the sands the land-locked waters lapped gently, shimmering with many colors. The dark hills rose about the jungle in green slopes mottled with brown and streaked here and there with tiny wisps of smoke.

I suddenly thought that the peaceful aspect of those hills was exactly what must have struck the men aboard the gunboat Euphrosyne when its opportune appearance had given Osa and me the chance for our lives. The memory of that horrible adventure made me momentarily uneasy. Osa squeezed my arm, and I knew that her thoughts, too, had gone back to the evening when, in the gathering darkness, we had slipped from the edge of the jungle, tattered, bleeding, and terrified, and rushed into the water pursued by the yelling savages.

Paul was not troubled by any forebodings. He at once suggested that we go ashore. So Osa and I followed him into the boat and we pulled for the beach, followed by the small boats from the other cutters. As we landed, about twenty armed savages suddenly appeared and came walking boldly toward us. Except for belts of rough bark and clouts of pandanus fiber, they were naked. The flatness of their noses was accentuated by plugs driven through the cartilage dividing the nostrils. Shaggy, outstanding manes of hair completely encircled their faces, which were deeply seamed and wore a perpetual scowl.

I began to doubt once more whether I could fulfill the object of my expedition after all. There was no man living who had witnessed the cannibalistic rites of these wild men. Many had made the attempt and had paid a gruesome penalty. But as the band drew nearer, my feeling changed. In a sense, they were my people. They had encircled the globe with me and in the comfortable surroundings of great theaters had stood naked and terrible before thousands of civilized people. I had made their faces familiar in all parts of the world. With something like emotion I watched them as they approached. Suddenly the figure at their head stood out like a "fade-in."

It was Nagapate.

Osa and I forgot that this savage had once wanted to eat us. We forgot what had happened at our first violent meeting. We looked at each other and smiled and then, both actuated by the same unaccountable impulse, we rushed forward and grabbed his hand.

Now Nagapate did not know the meaning of a handshake, but he seemed to understand instantly that we were glad to see him. His heavy face, gashed so deeply with wrinkles that his scowl seemed unalterable, broke into a delighted grin. He recovered his dignity in a moment, however, and stood to one side with his arms folded on his massive chest, watching closely every move we made. The strong guard we had brought with us must have impressed him; but he did not seem at all apprehensive, for he could tell by our conduct that we were friendly. We were anxious to get some pictures. However, since fresh relays of savages continued to come down from the jungle, we decided to wait until we had with us all the boys from the other boats before taking any further chances.

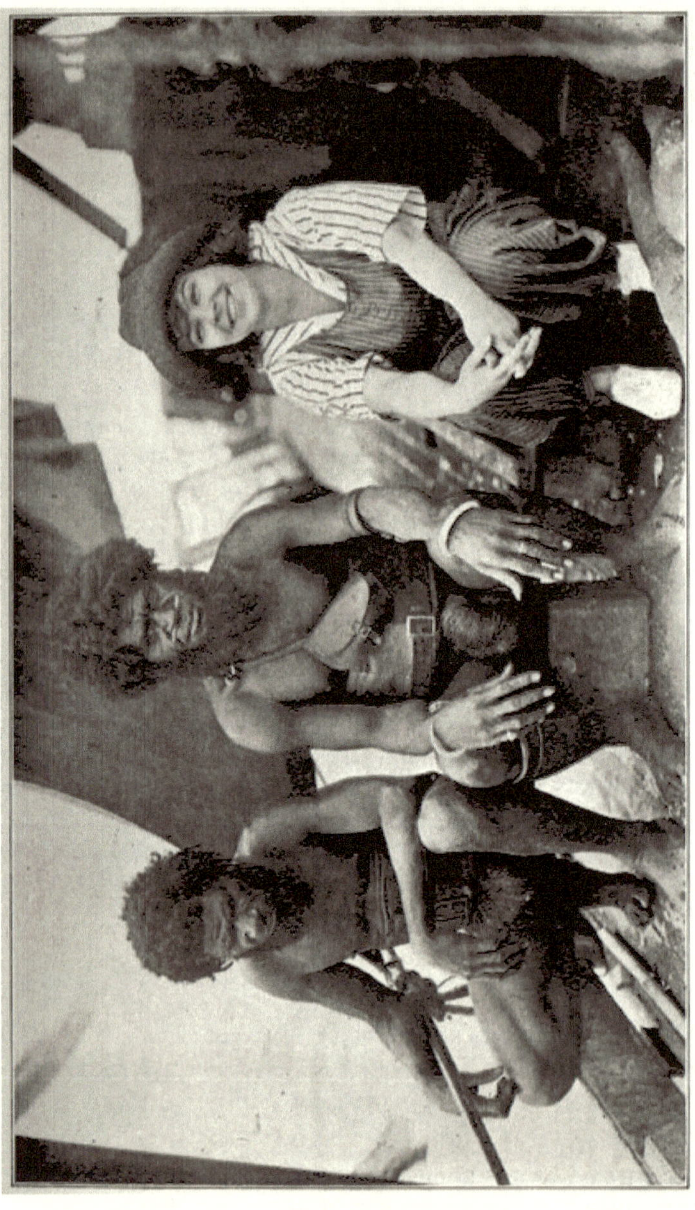

A CALL FROM NAGAPATE

We decided to return to the cutter, and as we were about to embark an extraordinary thing happened. Nagapate came up to Osa and made signs to show that he would like to go aboard with us. Now hundreds of his own people had been grabbed from his beach in times gone by and "blackbirded" away to slavery. He was accustomed, and with cause, to think the white man as merciless as we thought him to be. Yet of his own free will, without a glimmer of fear, Nagapate put himself completely in our power.

An hour later, while we ate our dinner of tinned beef, Nagapate, with two of his men, squatted on the deck at our feet and ate hard-tack and white trade-salmon. Afterwards I brought out pictures I had made on my first visit. The savages gave yells of excitement when they saw Nagapate's face caught on paper. When I produced a large colored poster of the chief and presented it to him, he was speechless. The three savages, looking at this mysterious likeness, were almost ready to kow-tow to us, as they did to their devil-devils in the bush.

But the crowning touch of all came when we had grown a little tired of our guests, and Osa brought out her ukulele and commenced to sing. To our surprise Nagapate joined in, chanting a weird melody, which his men took up. After a few bars, they were made shy by the sound of their own voices. Nagapate stopped his song and vainly tried once more to look dignified. In fact, that old man-eater showed every manifestation of a young and awkward boy's self-consciousness!

We bridged over the awkward situation with more salmon and about ten o'clock sent him ashore happy, with his bare arms full of knives and calico and tobacco. We judged by his farewell that we would be welcome any time we cared to drop in on him for dinner and that we had a fair prospect of not being served up as the main course. In any case, on the strength of his visit, I determined to chance a visit to his village on the following day, though I realized that the visit, in many ways significant, did not give the least assurance of continued friendliness. These savages are as willful and as uncertain in their moods as children. When they are sulky, they are as likely to murder treacherously whoever arouses their ill-will as a small boy is to throw a stone. There is no one to control or guide them. They are physically powerful, they are passionate, and they possess deadly weapons. We could be no more certain that our lives would be safe with them than a man with a silk hat can be sure of his headgear among three hundred schoolboys fighting with snowballs.

We were awakened at daybreak by a shout from the shore. A score of natives stood on the beach, calling and gesticulating. I went ashore, accompanied by Paul Mazouyer, and found that they had presents from their chief, Nagapate—yams and coconuts and wild fruits. But the presents were not for me. In their almost unintelligible *bêche-de-mer*, the natives explained that the fruits were for "Mary" — their *bêche-de-mer* word for woman. I could scarcely believe my ears. In all my experience among the blacks of the South Seas, I had never known a savage to pay any attention to a woman, except to beat her or to growl at her. The women of the islands are slaves, valued at so many pigs. They do all the work that is done in the native villages and get scoldings and kicks for thanks. I went doubtfully back to the schooner and brought Osa ashore. The natives greeted her with grunts of satisfaction and laid their offering at her feet.

My respect for Nagapate increased. I saw that he was a diplomat. He had observed that this little person in overalls, who had approached him so fearlessly, was treated with the utmost deference by the crews of the schooners and by the white men. He had come to the conclusion that she was the real boss of the expedition. And he was very nearly right!

Perrole and Stephens joined us, and we remained on the beach all morning. Osa and I took pictures of the natives squatting about us and watched for Nagapate himself to put in an appearance. I was eager to invite him to his first "movie." He had been overcome with awe at sight of a photograph of himself. What would he say to motion-pictures that showed him talking, with threatening gestures, and scowling as on that memorable day two years before?

Every now and then a new delegation of natives arrived on the beach. In spite of the law that prohibits the sale of firearms to the natives, they all carried rifles. I examined some of the guns. They were old, but not too old to do damage, and every native had a supply of cartridges. I found later that spears and bows and arrows are almost out of use among the Big Numbers. Nine men out of ten own guns. Where do they get them? No native will tell, for telling would mean no more rifles and no more cartridges. The white people of the islands know, but they keep their information to themselves. I know, too, but I am not doing any talking either, for I want to go back to the New Hebrides some day.

Our own boys remained close by us all the morning and we kept sharp watch for any sign of treachery. By noon, the savages had lost their suspicion of us. They stacked their rifles against rocks and trees and moved about, talking to each other in their strange, grunting speech. We, too, moved about more freely. And I tried to gain the confidence of the natives by talking to them. My attempts to learn their language with *bêche-de-mer* as a medium brought great guffaws. But in spite of the friendliness of our visitors, we were never quite at ease. Their appearance was against them. Their ugly faces—eyes with scarcely any pupils, flat noses made twice their normal size by the wooden plugs thrust through the cartilage dividing the nostrils, great mouths with thick, loose lips—their stealthy way of walking, their coarse, rapid, guttural speech, which sounded angry even when they spoke to one another, the quick gestures with which they filled in the gaps in their limited language—none of these things tended to make us feel at home.

I kept wondering how some of Osa's sheltered young friends back home would act, if they were to be set down, as she was, on a sandy beach, miles from civilization, and surrounded with fierce cannibals—hideous and worse than naked; for they worship sex, and what clothing they wear calls attention to their sex rather than conceals it. I watched her admiringly as she went about taking snapshots as unconcernedly as if the savages had been Boy Scouts on an outing. And I thought, as I have thought many many times in the nine years we have gone about together, how lucky I was. Osa has all the qualities that go to make an ideal traveling companion for an explorer—pluck, endurance, cheerfulness under discomfort. In an emergency, I would trust her far sooner than I would trust most men.

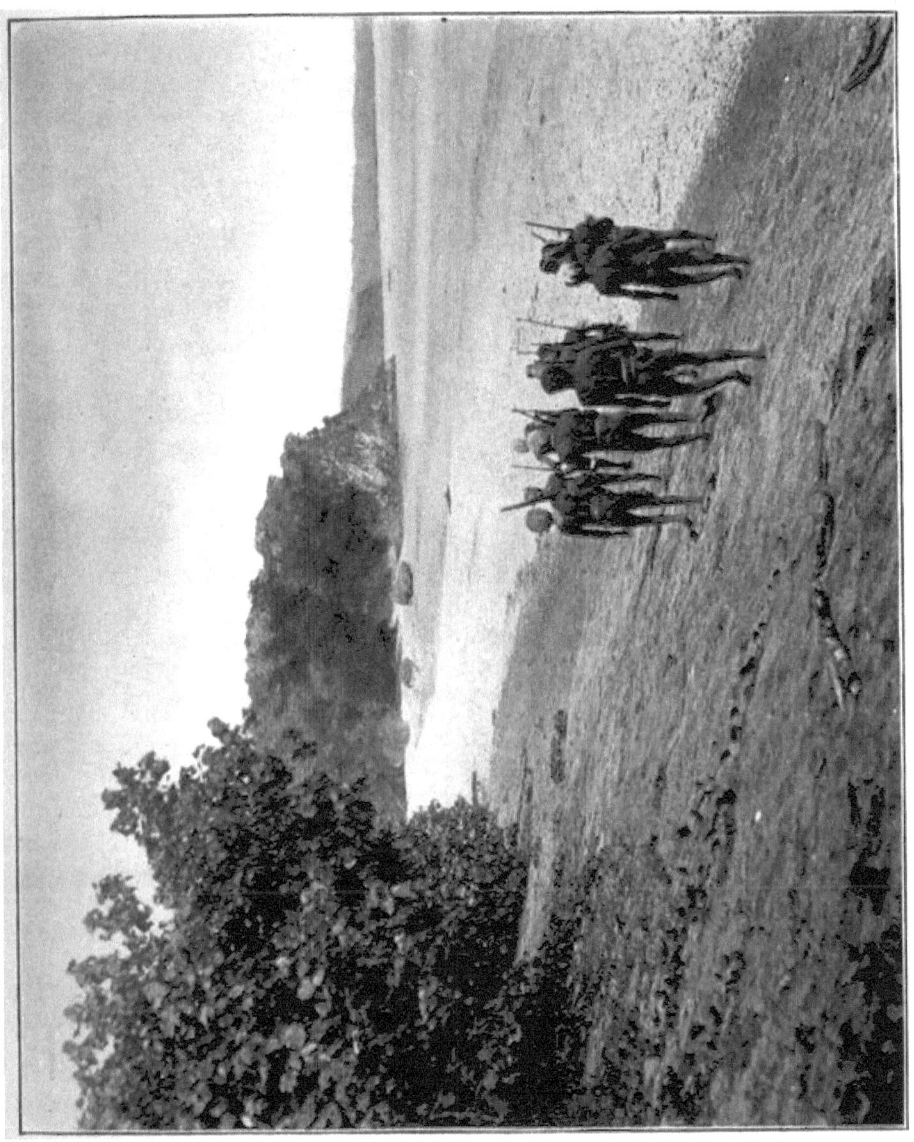

THE SAFE BEACH TRAIL, TANEMAROU BAY

During the afternoon, several fresh groups of natives came out of the jungle to stare at us, and toward sunset a number of savages descended a trail that sloped down to the beach about half a mile from where we were sitting and brought us a message from the great chief. It was couched as follows: "Nagapate, he big fellow master belong Big Numbers. He, he wantem you, you two fellow, you come along lookem house belong him, you lookem piccaninny belong him, you lookem Mary belong him. He makem big fellow sing-sing. More good you, you two fellow come. He no makem bad, he makem good altogether." And it meant that His

Highness, Chief Nagapate, would like to have us visit him in his village, and that he guaranteed our safety.

I accepted the invitation with alacrity. The messengers hurried off, and Osa and I followed, curious to see where the trail left the beach. We had not gone far, before Paul shouted for us to stop. We halted and saw, a quarter of a mile down the beach, a group of about a hundred armed natives. Some Big Numbers people came up to us and warned us, with gestures, to go no farther, so we sat down on the sand and awaited developments. The newcomers squatted on the beach and stared in our direction. In about fifteen minutes, a second group of natives appeared from a trail still farther down the beach, and the first group sprang to their feet and melted into the bush with incredible rapidity.

What did it all mean? Paul, well versed in island lore, had the answer. The beach was used jointly by four tribes, three belonging to the Big Numbers and one to the Small Numbers people. All of these tribes are more or less hostile, but they have agreed between them that the beach is neutral ground, for they realize that if fighting is permitted there, it will never be safe for any of them to come out into the open to trade or fish. Sometimes the beach armistice is violated, and for weeks there is severe fighting along the sand; in the end, however, the matter is always settled by an exchange of wild pigs and the beach is again safe for all comers. But the armistice never extends back into the bush. In the jungle and the tall cane-grass, it is always open season for man-killing.

We returned to the schooner early that evening, in order to make ready for our trip into the interior. I packed all my photographic apparatus carefully in canvas and rubber cases, and I bundled up several tarpaulins to protect us and our cameras in case of sudden rain. We put up enough supplies to last seven or eight days, and a good equipment of trade-stuffs. As we packed, the monotonous chanting of some twenty of Nagapate's men, who had remained on the beach to escort us to the village, drifted across the water. Occasionally we caught a glimpse of them, grotesque black shapes against the light from their camp-fire.

CHAPTER V

IN NAGAPATE'S KINGDOM

Next morning, before daybreak, we were on the beach. The embers of the camp-fire remained, but our escort had vanished. I was filled with misgivings. Did Nagapate plan treachery? We were thirty-one—twenty-six trustworthy native boys, four white men, and Osa. We were all well equipped with repeating rifles and automatic pistols. In open fight, we could have stood off a thousand savages. But I knew that the men of Malekula, though they are notoriously bad shots, could pick us off one by one, if they wished, as we went through the jungle.

I suppose that we all felt a little doubtful about taking the plunge into the jungle, but we all—with the exception of our native boys, who were plainly in a blue funk—kept our doubts to ourselves. The boys were so frightened that they rebelled against carrying anything except their guns. To inspire them with confidence, each of us took a piece of luggage, and then we divided among them what was left and persuaded them to take the trail.

It was dawn on the beach, but it was still night in the jungle. The trail was a dark tunnel with walls and roof of underbrush and trees and tangled vines. We stumbled along blindly at first. Presently our eyes became used to the dark and we walked with more ease. Stems and thorns caught at our clothes as we passed. We slipped on wet, slimy roots and stumbled over them in the dim light. Only where the jungle was intersected by one of the numerous streams—swift but shallow and never too wide for leaping—that water the island, did the light succeed in struggling weakly through the tangle.

The New Hebridean jungle is different from that of India or Africa. The severe hurricanes that sweep over the islands each year have stunted growth. There are no forest giants. Trees send their branches out rather than up, forming a dense mass of vegetation that is further bound together by vines, so that it is almost impossible to penetrate the jungle save by beaten trails or along the courses of streams.

The sun was well up when we came out on the first of a series of plateaus that formed a giant stairway up the mountain. They were separated from one another by five hundred to a thousand yards of scrub trees and tangled bush. It was not easy going. The ascents were steep, and the trail was wet and slippery.

We kept watch for treacherous natives. Once we were startled by blood-curdling cries that came from the direction in which we were going. Our boys said the men of Malekula were hunting wild pigs. We went on in silence. Our hearts jumped every time a twig cracked. There was a set expression on Osa's face. I knew she was frightened, but I knew, too, that no amount of money would have persuaded her to turn back.

By noon we had reached what seemed to be the highest point of northern Malekula, and looked back over valley after valley of dense jungle, and plateau after plateau covered with cane-grass. Here and there a coconut tree stood out alone. Smoke, curling out of the hillsides, indicated the sites of native villages. Perhaps, at that very moment, gruesome feasts of human flesh were being prepared. In the bay, very small and very far off, were three black dots—our boats.

We heard a sound behind us and quickly turned. There were some twenty men, sent by the "big fellow master belong Big Numbers." They took our apparatus and indicated that we were to follow them. We were dead tired; still there seemed nothing to do but to push on.

We were not sorry, after about a mile, to approach a village. First we came upon scattered groves of coconut and banana trees. Our trail became wider and harder and we passed weed-grown patches of yams and taro, protected against the wild pigs by rude walls of bamboo. Finally we came out upon a clearing around which clustered a few wretched shelters thatched roughly with leaves. In the center of the clearing stood upright hollow logs—the drums used to send messages from village to village and to furnish music for the native dances. The natives called them boo-boos—the name given to conch-shells and all other sound-making instruments. On the hard ground of the clearing sat some thirty savages, all well armed. They had apparently been watching for us, but they did not greet us. We spoke to them, but, beyond a few grunts, they made no reply. There were no women and children in sight. That was a bad sign; for the women and children are sent away only when there is trouble in the air. Perrole, Stephens, and Mazouyer drew nearer to Osa and me. Their faces were grave. Our boys edged close to us. None of us spoke.

After a short rest, our guides indicated that we were to take the trail again. We pushed on over a muddy path, bordered by coconut and banana trees, and in about fifteen minutes we came out upon another clearing, much larger than the first, with many more huts surrounding it and with more and bigger boo-boos in the center. Here again were savages awaiting us—about two hundred of them, each with a gun. We were led to a big boo-boo that had been overturned by the wind and were told to sit down. We obeyed like obedient school-children.

One of the natives beat out on a boo-boo an irregular boom-boom-boom that roared through the clearing and was echoed back from the hills. It sounded like a code. We felt that it might be a summons to the executioner. Osa huddled close to me. A stillness fell over the assembly.

Suddenly, at the far side of the clearing, a huge savage appeared. It was Nagapate. He stood for a moment, looking over the audience; then he walked slowly and majestically into the center of the clearing. He roared a few words to his men. Then he turned to us. A native came running up—the laziest black stepped lively when Nagapate commanded—with a block of wood for a throne. The chief sat down near us, and we stepped forward and shook hands with him. He had grown used to this form of greeting and responded with graciousness.

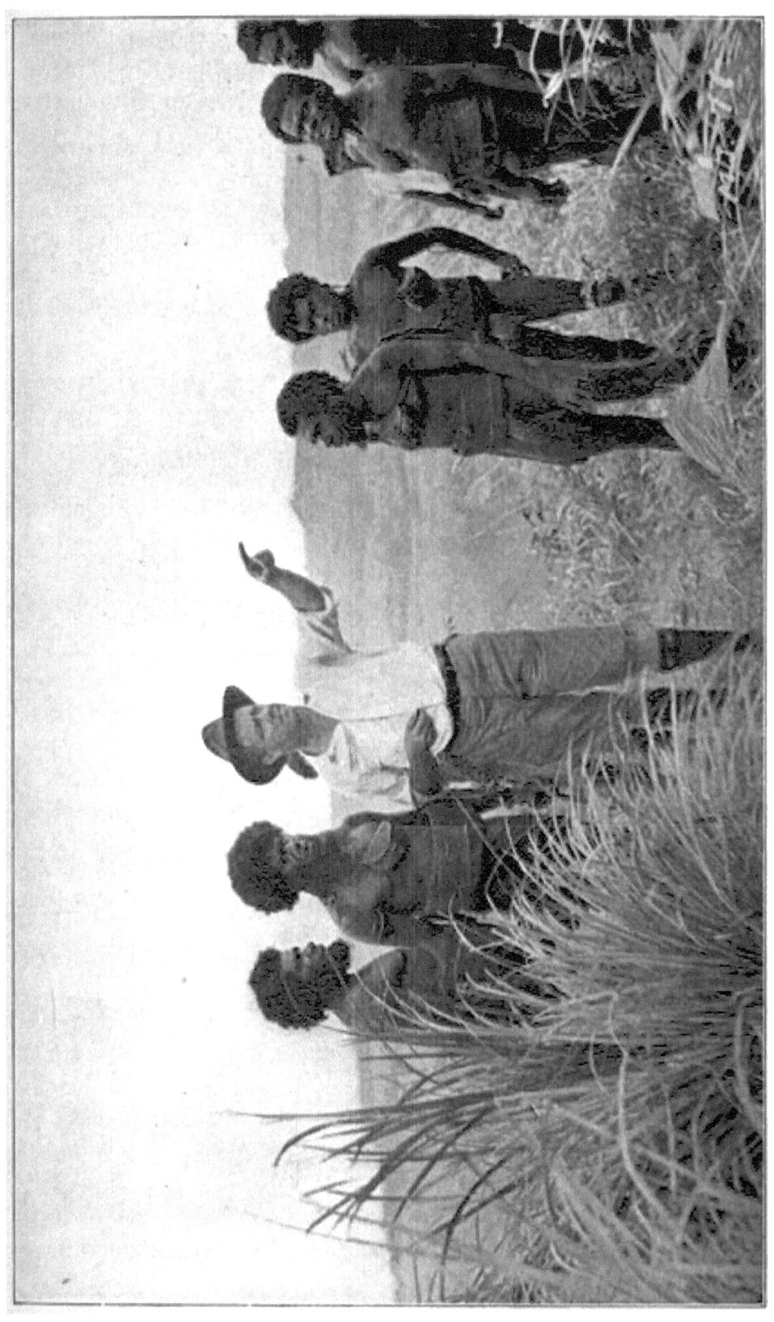

LOOKING OVER NAGAPATE'S KINGDOM FROM THE HIGHEST PEAK IN NORTHERN MALEKULA

It had been a wonderful entrance. But then Nagapate had an instinct for the dramatic. Throughout our stay in his village, I noticed, he never made a move that was not staged. He let it be known by his every act that he was no common chief, who had won his position through skill in killing pigs or men. Nagapate was a king and a descendant of kings. His was the only tribe I had come across during my travels among the blacks of the South Pacific that had an hereditary ruler.

After he had greeted us, he uttered a sharp command and a native stepped up with a big bamboo water-bottle. Nagapate drank from it, and then the native offered it, tilted at the proper angle, to each of us in turn. It was not pleasant to drink from the mouthpiece at which Nagapate's great lips had sucked. But we gathered that the bottle was the South Sea equivalent of a pipe of peace; so we drank gladly. I then presented to Nagapate a royal gift of knives, calico, and tobacco, and I told one of the boys to give two sticks of tobacco to each native.

The natives smoked their tobacco (those that did not eat it) at once and greedily. It seemed to break the ice a bit; so I got out my cameras. For three hours, I made pictures. But I did not get any "action." I wanted a picture of a man coming out of his house; for the doors of the huts are so low that the people have to come out on all fours. I persuaded a native to go into his hut and come out again. He did so. But his companions laughed and jeered at him, and after that every one had stage fright.

As the afternoon wore on, scores of women and children appeared. I have never seen human beings more wretched than those women. At first sight they looked like walking haystacks. They wore dresses of purple dyed grasses, consisting of a bushy skirt that hung from the waist to the knees, a sort of widow's veil that was thrown over the head and face so as to leave a tiny peep-hole for the wearer to look through, and a long train that hung down the back nearly to the ground. A more cumbersome and insanitary dress was never devised. It was heavy. It was hot. Worst of all, it was dirty. Every one of the dresses was matted with filth. I did not see a single pig—and there were dozens of them rooting about inside and outside the houses—that was so dirty as the women of that village. I afterward found that for women to wash was strictly taboo. From birth to death water never touched their skins!

I got my cameras ready, but the women hid in the houses and would not come out to be photographed. Not until Nagapate commanded them to come into the clearing did they creep whimpering in terror from the low doors.

We had heard from the natives at our headquarters on the island of Vao that Nagapate had a hundred wives, but there were only ten of them, and they were as wretched as any of the other women. Osa presented them each with a string of beads and a small glass jar of cheap candy. They did not even look at their gifts. They wanted only to get the ordeal over and to escape. During all our stay in the village the poor, browbeaten wretches never got up enough courage to look at us. Their lords and masters felt our skins and our hair and our clothes, examining us with embarrassing freedom. But whenever we came upon a woman, she squatted down and hid her face behind her grass veil.

Since the women and children had appeared, we gained confidence and walked about the village, inspecting the houses. As we approached, the children, scrawny little wretches, big-bellied from malnutrition and many of them covered with sores, scurried off into the bush like frightened rabbits. The houses were wretched huts made of poles with a covering of leaves and grass, or, occasionally, of woven bamboo. Inside were the embers of fires—nothing more. A hard, worn place on the ground in one corner showed where the owner slept. Nagapate's house stood off by itself. It was larger than the rest and more compactly made. But it was as bare as any of the others.

Toward sunset we built a fire and cooked our supper. The natives gathered around and watched us in astonishment. They themselves made no such elaborate preparation for eating. Once in a while a man would kindle a fire and throw a few yams among the coals. When the yams were burned black on one side, he would turn them with a stick and burn them on the other. Then they were ready for eating—the outside burned crisp and the inside raw. One evening some of the men brought in some little pigs, broke their legs, so that they could not escape, and threw them, squealing, into a corner of a hut. The next day there was meat to eat. Like the yams, it was only half-cooked. The natives tore it with their teeth as if they had been animals, and they seemed especially to relish the crisp, burned portions. Each man was his own cook. Even Nagapate made his own fire and cooked his own food, for it was taboo for him to eat anything prepared by an inferior or cooked over a fire made by an inferior. He conveniently considered us his superiors and ate greedily everything we gave him. He never shared the salmon and rice he got from us either with his cronies or with his wives. In fact, we never saw a woman eating, and the children seemed to live on sugar-cane and on clay that they dug up with their skinny little fingers.

Our first day as Nagapate's guests drew to an end. Just before dark a native came and motioned to us to follow him. He led us to a new house and indicated that we were to make ourselves at home there. We were tired out after our long march; so we turned in without delay. We spread our blankets on the ground and lay, fully dressed, on top of them. The camp soon became quiet, but we could not sleep. So far, everything had gone well, but still we did not feel quite safe. Our boys seemed to share our apprehension. They crowded around the hut, as close to us as they could get. Some of them slipped under the grass walls and lay half inside the hut.

We slept little and were up before dawn, stiff from lying on the hard ground. We asked for water, and a native brought it in a bamboo bottle. There was about a pint of water for each of the five of us. The savage that brought it looked on astonished as we washed our hands and faces. It is not taboo for the Big Numbers men to bathe—but they rarely use their privilege, and they could not understand our reckless waste of water, which was carried by the women from a spring half a mile away.

After a breakfast of tinned beef, we set to work. But if it had been hard to get good pictures the day before, it was now almost impossible. The women had all left the village to get the day's supply of water, fruits, and firewood. The men squatted in the center of the clearing, guns in hand. They were apparently waiting for something—for what?

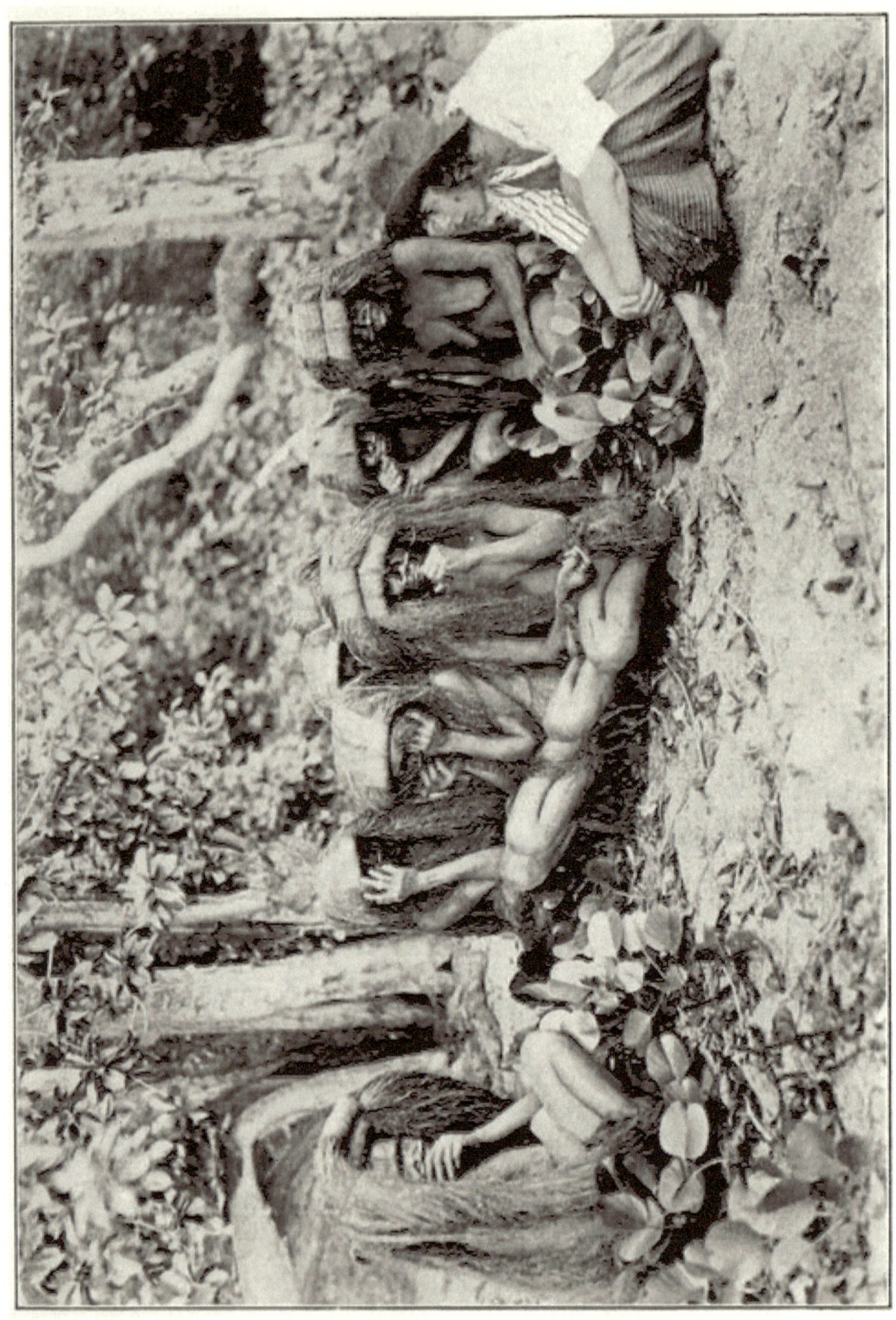

WOMEN OF THE BIG NUMBERS

We were uneasy. It may seem to the reader, in view of the fact that we escaped with whole skins, that we were absurdly uneasy. But I should like to see the man who could remain calm when surrounded as we were by savages, ugly and powerful, whose only pleasure was murder, and who, we were convinced, were eaters of human flesh. All day long our hosts squatted about the giant boo-boos, staring at us or at the ground or at the jungle or, sometimes, it seemed, at nothing at all. Now and then a single savage would come out of the jungle and join the group, and immediately one of the squatters would get up and go into the bush, taking the trail by which the newcomer had arrived. Even Paul was troubled, and confided to me, when the others were not about, "Me no like."

The coming and going and interminable squatting and staring got on the nerves of all of us. Toward evening, we received an explanation of it from Atree, Nagapate's "private secretary." Atree had been "blackbirded" away from the island about twelve years previous to our arrival, in the days when natives were still carried off by force for servitude on the plantations of Queensland; and, by some miracle, when the all-white Australia law had gone into effect and the blacks had been "repatriated," he had made his way back to his own island. He had managed, during his sojourn abroad, to pick up a little *bêche-de-mer*; so he acted as go-between and interpreter in all our dealings with Nagapate. He told us that a fight with a neighboring village was brewing. There had been a dispute over some pigs, in which somebody had got hurt. The relatives of the victim were preparing to attack our hosts. The men who had come and gone from the clearing were the lookouts who guarded the village against surprise.

A fight! My first thought was, "What a picture I'll get!" But Osa, at my elbow, said miserably, "I wish we were back in the boat," and my conscience began to hurt. To reassure her I told her that our force was a match for half a dozen native villages.

Before sunset there was great activity in the clearing. Men kept coming and going, and there was much grunted consultation in the shadow of the boo-boos. All that night an armed guard stood watch.

At sunrise, Nagapate came and asked if we would shoot off our guns to frighten the enemy. I did not like the idea. I thought it might be a ruse to get us to empty our guns and to give the natives a chance to rush on us before we could reload. However, since we did not wish to seem suspicious, we granted the request. But we fired in rotation, instead of in a volley, so that there would always be some among us with ready rifles. And I found that I was not the only one who had thought of the danger of empty cartridge-chambers: I have never seen such snappy reloading as that of our black boys!

After the volley, I gave Nagapate my rifle to shoot. He unloaded her as fast as he could pull the trigger, and begged for more, like an eager small boy. I was sorry to refuse him, but I did not care to waste many cartridges, so I explained through Atree that the gun had to cool off, and Nagapate, to my relief, seemed satisfied with the explanation.

After the shooting was over, everybody seemed to take courage. The natives moved about more freely. Only about a third remained armed and ready for summons. They were apparently satisfied that their enemies, convinced that they were well supplied with ammunition, would be afraid to start hostilities. We ourselves were more at ease, and I went up to some of the soldiers and examined their fighting equipment. Their guns were, as usual, old and rusty, but they all had cartridges, which they carried in leather cartridge cases slung over their shoulders. I was surprised to find that none had clubs. Instead, they had big knives, some of them three feet long, for hand-to-hand fighting. Paul told me that such knives had become the most sought-for articles of trade. There was no Government ban on them as on rifles and cartridges.

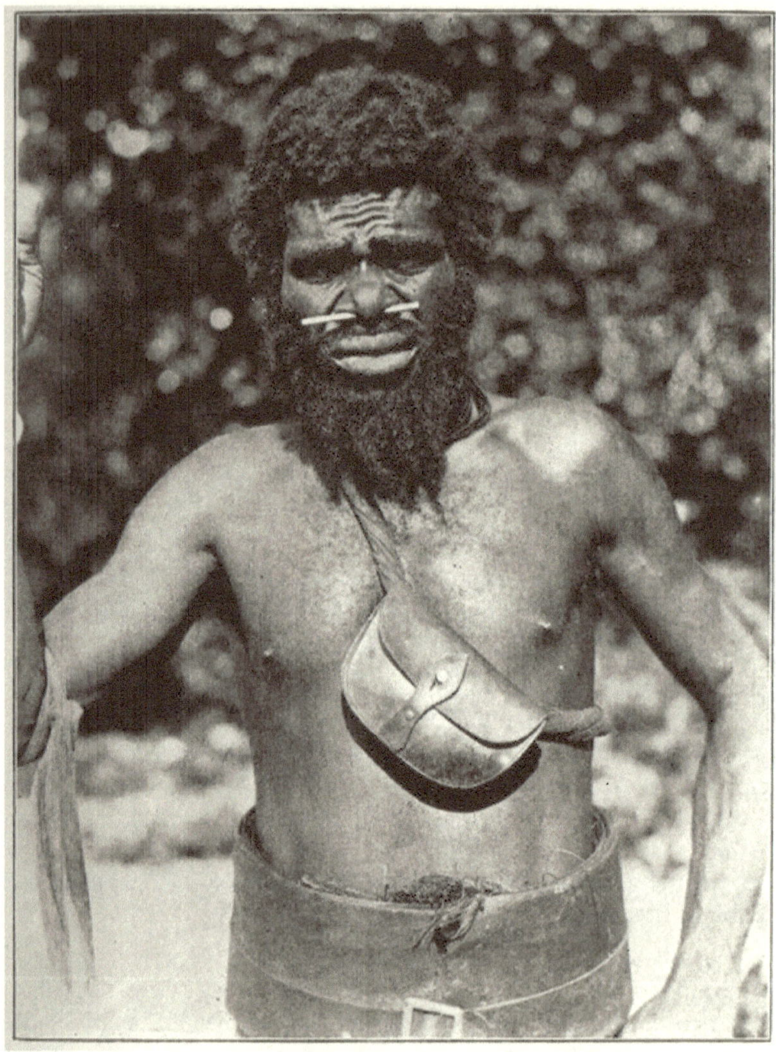

RAMBI

On the afternoon of our fourth day in the village, Nagapate brought up a man we had not seen before. He was nearly as large as Nagapate himself, and had, like Nagapate, an air of commanding dignity.

"Rambi! Rambi!" growled Nagapate, pointing to his companion. Then the chief went through a rapid pantomime, in which he seemed to kill off a whole army of enemies. We gathered that Rambi was minister of war, as indeed he was; but Osa dubbed him chief of police. We learned from Paul that the tribe was ruled by a sort of triumvirate, with Nagapate in supreme command and Rambi and a third chief named Velle-Velle, who acted as a primitive prime minister, next in authority.

Rambi was a Godsend. He enjoyed being photographed, although he did not have the slightest idea of what the operation meant. He forgot his dignity and capered like a monkey in front of my camera and actually succeeded in injecting a little enthusiasm into the rest of the natives, who still suffered from stage fright.

I gave presents of tobacco for every picture I made. I must have paid out several dollars' worth of tobacco each day. Ten years earlier, when I was on the Snark with Jack London, trade tobacco made from the stalks and refuse from the Virginia tobacco factories had cost less than a cent a stick. The supply I had with me in Malekula had cost almost four cents a stick. Thus the high cost of living makes itself felt even in the South Seas. Tinned foods, cartridges, gasoline, mirrors, knives, and calico also have increased in price enormously since the war. An explorer must expect his expenses to be just about four hundred per cent higher than they were ten years ago. And the trader is in a bad way. For the natives learned how to value trade-stuffs years ago and they insist on buying at the old rate. Increased costs and greater difficulty of transportation mean nothing to them.

On the next day, we went, with an escort of several of Nagapate's men, to another Big Numbers village about four miles away. That trip was typical of the many downs that are mingled with the ups in a motion-picture man's existence. The four miles were the hardest four miles I ever walked. The trail lay along the side of a hill, following a deep valley. It was seldom used, and it slanted toward the valley in an alarming way. It was slimy with mud and decayed vegetation, and in many places a slip would have meant a slide of several hundred feet down a steep hill. Both Osa and I had on spiked boots, but they soon became clogged with mud and offered less grip than ordinary shoes. We crept along at a snail's pace, testing every foothold. Though we left Nagapate's village at dawn, we did not reach our destination until after ten o'clock. It was a poor and uninteresting village of about thirty houses. Most of the men were off on a pig hunt, and all the women were out collecting firewood and fruits and vegetables. About noon, it began to drizzle. By three o'clock, it had settled down to a good downpour. The women straggled in one by one and retreated into their houses. The men returned in a sullen humor, with a few skinny pigs. According to custom, they broke one hind leg and one front leg of each animal to prevent its escape and threw the wretched little creatures in a squalling, moaning heap. Those on the bottom probably suffocated before morning.

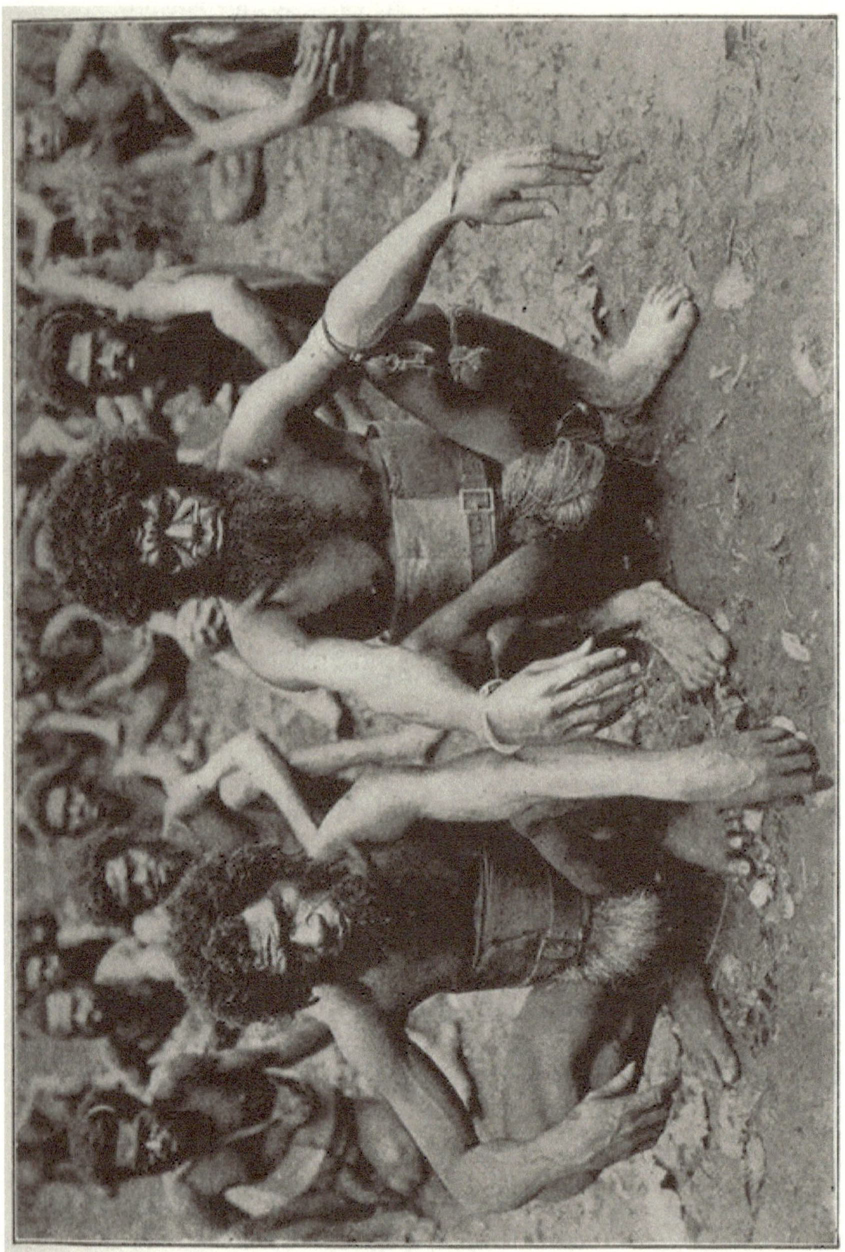

ATREE AND NAGAPATE

We could not think of retracing our steps over the treacherous trail in that downpour; so we persuaded a native and his wife and two sore-faced children to give up their hut to us. Since we had no blankets, we lay on the hard ground and made the best of a bad bargain.

Next morning, the rain had ceased. But the cane-grass was as wet as a sponge. We had not gone a hundred yards toward Nagapate's village before we were soaked through. The trail was more slippery than ever. About every quarter of a mile we had to stop and rest. The sun came out boiling hot and sucked up the moisture, which rose like steam all about us. We were five hours in this natural Turkish bath. When we reached our destination, we threw ourselves down and fell asleep in sheer exhaustion. We had not secured a single foot of film, and we felt miserably that we stood a very good chance of contracting fever, which so far we had luckily escaped.

Late that afternoon, I missed Osa. I had something of a hunt for her, but I finally found her in the shade at the edge of the clearing, playing with a little naked piccaninny. Atree and Nagapate squatted near by, watching her with grave, intent faces.

Nagapate was Osa's constant companion. The great chief had taken a fancy to the white "Mary." Every day he sent her gifts, and his yams and fruits and coconuts pleased her more than if they had been expensive presents of civilization. They seemed to her an assurance of his good-will. But the rest of us were a bit uneasy. We had what I now believe to be the absurd suspicion that all these gifts were tokens of savage wooing—that perhaps Nagapate was planning to massacre us, if the occasion offered, and keep Osa to share his wretched hut. The strain of constant watching, constant suspicion, was telling on our nerves. We fancied that the novelty of our presence was wearing off. Like children, the savages soon weary of a diversion. We were becoming familiar—dangerously familiar—to them, and our gifts and even the magic taught me by the great Houdini, had begun to pall. We began to feel that it was time for us to go.

Osa and I talked it over as we walked about the village the following afternoon. We strayed farther than usual and suddenly found ourselves near what seemed to be a deserted hut. We walked around it and found, on the far side, a well-beaten path that led to a tiny door. Without thinking, I crawled through the doorway, and Osa followed me. It was several seconds before our eyes became accustomed to the dim light. Suddenly Osa gasped and clutched my arm.

All about us, piled in baskets, were dried human heads. A ghastly frieze of them grinned about the eaves. Skulls hung from the rafters, heaps of picked human bones lay in the corners. One glance was enough for us. We crawled out of the hut and lost no time in getting back to the center of the village. Luckily none of the savages had seen us.

We gathered Paul Mazouyer and Perrole and Stephens about us and told them of our adventure, and it did not take the conference long to decide to return to the beach on the following day. The other white men told us that if we had been seen in or near the head-house, the chances were that we should all have been murdered, for such houses were sacred and taboo to all, save the men of the village.

That evening a great fire was started in the clearing. Until late in the night the ordinarily lazy savages piled on great logs that four men were required to carry. Nothing was cooked over the fire. It was not needed for warmth, for the night was stifling hot. We asked Arree the reason for the illumination. He replied that he did not know. We decided that there must be some sinister purpose in it and lay sleepless, on guard the night through.

At dawn we were up. We did our packing in a hurry, and then we sent one of the natives for Nagapate. The chief came across the clearing, slowly and deliberately, as always. With him was a tottering old man, the oldest native I ever saw in the New Hebrides.

As Osa and I went up to greet Nagapate, the old man began to jabber excitedly. He came over to me and felt my arms and legs with both his skinny hands. He pinched me and poked me in the ribs and stomach. All the time he kept up a running fire of excited comment, addressed to Nagapate. To our relief, he finally stopped talking for want of breath. Nagapate spoke a few sharp words and the old man backed away.

Osa's face went white. And indeed, there could be no doubt about the meaning of the old native's pantomime. I almost doubted the advisability of telling Nagapate of our departure. If he liked, he could prevent us from ever reaching the sea, from which we were separated by so many miles of jungle. But I decided to take a chance. I had, by this time, rather more than a smattering of the language of Nagapate's tribe. I always make it a practice, when among new tribes, to learn four words—"Yes," "no," "good," and "bad." The language spoken by Nagapate and his followers was so primitive and contained so many repetitions that I had been able to progress beyond these four fundamental words and so, with the aid of gestures, I succeeded in telling Nagapate that our provisions had run out and that we had to return to our boats. To my surprise Nagapate not only assented to our departure, but volunteered to accompany us to the beach.

I invited the entire village to come to the beach for motion-pictures and tobacco, after sunset, on the following evening. Motion-pictures meant nothing to them; but tobacco they understood. So they agreed to come. We left like honored guests, with an escort of twenty-five savages. Nagapate himself walked (as a result of my maneuvering) safe between Osa and myself.

It had taken twelve hours to climb up to Nagapate's village. The return journey required only three. It was a pleasant morning's walk. The sun was shining bright and beautiful, many-colored birds fluttered about us.

When we arrived at the beach, we invited Nagapate and his boon companions, Atree and Rambi, to come on board the schooner. There we feasted them on hard-tack and white salmon. When bedtime came, the great chief indicated that it was his pleasure to sleep on board. I was heartily astonished and a little ashamed. After all our suspicions, Nagapate was again voluntarily putting himself into our hands, with the touching confidence of a little child.

Our royal guest and his men bunked in the engine-room. I happened to wake about midnight and took a peep at them. There they were, flat on their backs on the hard, greasy floor, sleeping like logs.

CHAPTER VI

THE BIG NUMBERS SEE THEMSELVES ON THE SCREEN

Early on the morning of the show, we got the whaleboats to work and took all my projection machinery ashore. Soon I had everything set up, ready for the show. But when I tried out the projector to see if it was shipshape, I found that my generator was out of order. Work as I would, I could not get a light. I was blue and discouraged. I had been looking forward to this show for two years, and now, apparently, it was not going to come off. Imagine going back several hundred thousand years and showing men of the Stone Age motion-pictures of themselves. That is what I had planned to do. For the men of Malekula are in the stage of development reached by our own ancestors long before the dawn of written history. Through my pictures of them, I had carried New York audiences back into the Stone Age. Now I wanted to transport the savages into 1919—and my generator would not work.

The projector was worked by man-power. Two men on each side turned the handles attached to the machinery that should produce the magic light; but though my boys ground patiently all afternoon, not a glimmer showed. Finally, I gave up and motioned them to stop. They misunderstood me and, thinking that I wanted them to turn faster, went to work with redoubled energy. The miracle happened— the light flashed on. In my excitement, I forgot my supper.

The beach was already crowded with savages. I had thought they might be curious about my machinery. But they scarcely looked at it. They just squatted on the sands with their guns clutched tight in their hands. No women and only three or four children accompanied them. In spite of my promise of tobacco, they had not quite trusted my invitation and they were on the lookout for foul play. By dark they were restless. They had received no tobacco. They did not understand all this preparation that culminated in nothing. They wanted action.

I saw that the show must begin at once; so I tested everything once more. Since I had no idea how the pictures would be received, I stationed armed guards at each side of the screen and around the projector, at points from which they could cover the audience. Then I tried to persuade my visitors to sit in front of the projector, where they would get a good view of the screen. They were now thoroughly suspicious and would not stay where I put them. They wanted to keep an eye on me. They were so uneasy that I expected to see them disappear into the bush at any moment. But Osa saved the situation. She took Nagapate by the arm and made him sit down beside her. The rest of the savages gathered about them. Then the show began.

First, a great bright square flashed on the screen. Then came a hundred feet of titles. The attention of the natives was divided between the strange letters and the rays of white light that passed above their heads. They looked forward and up and back toward me, jabbering all the time. Then slowly, out of nothing, a familiar form took shape on the screen. It was Osa, standing with bent head. The savages were silent with amazement. Here was Osa sitting at Nagapate's side—and there she was on the screen. The picture-Osa raised her head and winked at them. Pandemonium broke loose. "Osa—Osa—Osa—Osa," shouted the savages. They roared with laughter and screamed like rowdy children.

I had been afraid that my guests would be frightened and bolt at the first demonstration of my "magic," but they had been reassured by the familiar sight of Osa. Now they were ready for anything. I showed them a picture of Osa and me as we left the Astor Hotel in New York. Then I showed them the crazy thousands that had crowded New York streets on Armistice Day. I followed this picture with glimpses of Chicago, San Francisco, Los Angeles, Honolulu, Tokyo, and Sydney. Nagapate told me afterward that he had not known there were so many white people in all the world and asked me if the island I came from was much larger than Malekula. I showed in quick succession, steamers, racing automobiles, airplanes, elephants, ostriches, giraffes. The savages were silent; they could not comprehend these things. So I brought them nearer home, with pictures taken on Vao, Santo, and other islands of the New Hebrides.

Now it was time for the great scene. I instructed Paul in turning the crank of the projector and put Stephens and Perrole in charge of the radium flares. I myself took my stand behind my camera, which was trained on the audience. A hundred feet of titles—then Nagapate's face appeared suddenly on the screen. A great roar of "Nagapate" went up. At that instant the radium lights flashed on, and I, at my camera, ground out the picture of the cannibals at the "movies." True, about two thirds of the audience, terrified by the flares, made precipitately for the bush. But Nagapate and the savages around him sat pat and registered fear and amazement for my camera. In about two minutes the flares burned out. Then we coaxed back to their places the savages that had fled. I started the reel all over and ran it to the end amid an uproar that made it impossible for me to make myself heard when I wanted to speak to Osa. Practically every savage pictured on the screen was in the audience. In two years they had not changed at all, except, as Osa said, for additional layers of dirt. As each man appeared, they called out his name and laughed and shouted with joy. Among the figures that came and went on the screen was that of a man who had been dead a year. The natives were awe-struck. My magic could bring back the dead!

Midway in the performance I turned the projection handle over to Mazouyer and joined the audience. Osa was crying with excitement. And there was a lump in my own throat. We had looked forward a long time to this.

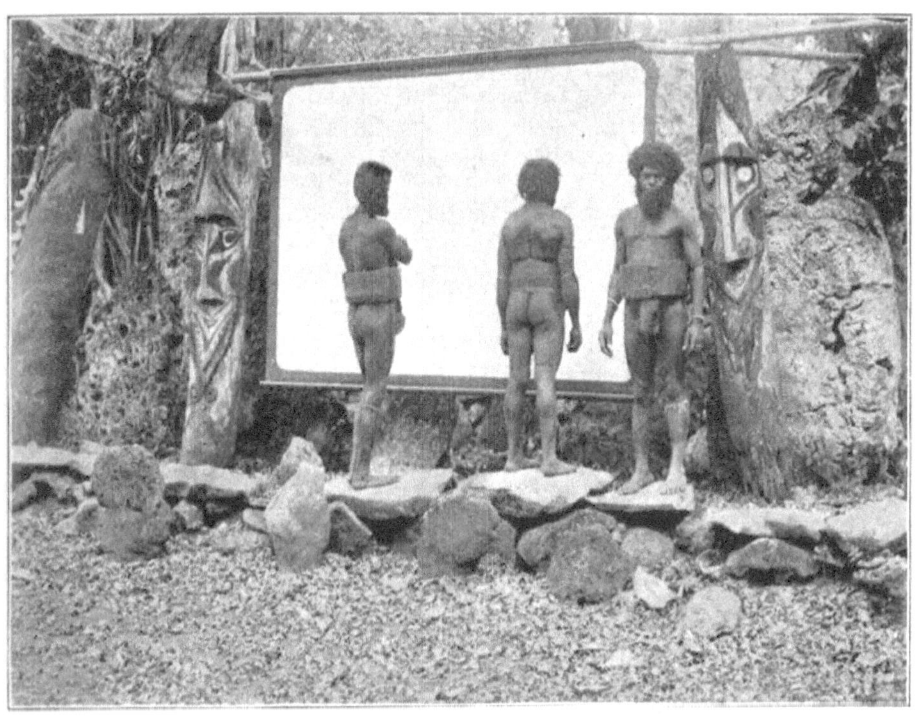

HUNTING FOR THE MAGIC

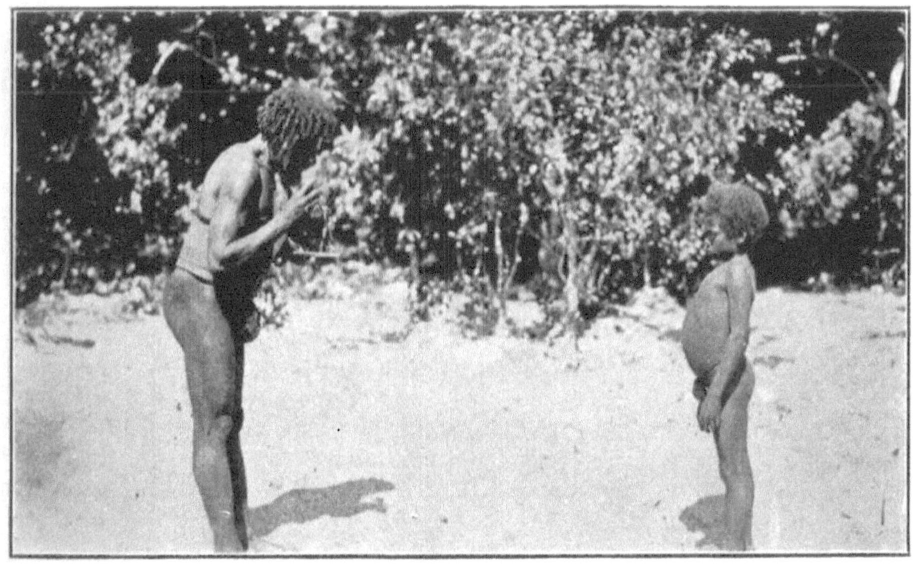

A CANNIBAL AND A KODAK

When the show was over, a great shout went up. The savages gathered into groups and discussed the performance, for all the world as people do "back home." Then they crowded about us, demanding their pay for looking at my pictures! As I gave them their sticks of tobacco, each grunted out the same phrase—whether it meant "Fine," or "Thank you," or just "Good-bye," I do not know.

While we packed our apparatus, the natives cut bamboo and made rude torches. When all were ready, they lighted their torches at the fire that burned on the beach, and then they set off in single file up the trail. We said good-bye to Perrole and Stephens, who were to sail for Santo that night, and prepared to go aboard Paul's cutter. He had difficulty in getting his engine started, and while he worked with it, Osa and I sat on the beach, watching the torches of the Big Numbers people as they filed up hill and down dale the long eight miles to their village. The night was so dark that we could not see anything except the string of lights that wound through the black like a fiery serpent. The head disappeared over the top of the hill. Half an hour later, the tail wriggled out of sight. Then the engine kicked off.

CHAPTER VII

THE NOBLE SAVAGE

The morning after our motion-picture show on the beach at Malekula found us anchored off Vao. We got our luggage ashore as quickly as possible and then turned in to make up for lost sleep. We had slept little during our eight days in the village of Nagapate. We had been in such constant fear of treachery that the thud of a falling coconut or the sound of a branch crackling in the jungle would set our nerves atingle and keep us awake for hours. Now we felt safe. We knew that the four hundred savages of Vao, though at heart as fierce and as cruel as any of the Malekula tribes, lived in wholesome fear of the British gunboat; so we slept well and long.

The next morning we said good-bye to Paul Mazouyer and he chugged away to Santo in the little schooner that for two weeks had been our home. Osa and I were alone on Vao. We turned back to our bungalow to make things comfortable, for we did not know how many days it would be before Mr. King, who had promised to call for us, would appear.

As we walked slowly up from the beach, we heard a shout. We turned and saw a savage running toward us. He was a man of about forty; yet he was little larger than a child and as naked as when he was born. From his almost unintelligible *bêche-de-mer*, we gathered that he wanted to be our servant. We could scarcely believe our ears. Here was a man who wanted to work! We wondered how he came to have a desire so contrary to Vao nature, until we discovered, after a little further conversation in *bêche-de-mer*, that he was half-witted! Since we were in need of native help, we decided not to let his mental deficiencies stand in his way and we hired him on the spot. Then came the first hitch. We could not find out his name. Over and over, we asked him, "What name belong you?" but with no result. He shook his head uncomprehendingly. Finally, Osa pointed to the tracks he had left in the sand. They led down to the shore and vanished at the water's edge. "His name is Friday," she said triumphantly. And so we called him.

From that moment, Friday was a member of our household. We gave him a singlet and a *lava-lava*, or loin-cloth, of red calico, and from somewhere he dug up an ancient derby hat. Some mornings he presented himself dressed in nothing but the hat. He was always on hand bright and early, begging for work, but, unfortunately, there was nothing that he could do. We tried him at washing clothes, and they appeared on the line dirtier than they had been before he touched them. We tried him at carrying water, but he brought us liquid mud, with sticks and leaves floating on the top. The only thing he was good for was digging bait and paddling the canoe gently to keep it from drifting while Osa fished.

That was, indeed, a service of some value; for Osa was an indefatigable fisherwoman. Every day, she went out and brought back from ten to thirty one- and two-pound fish, and one day she caught two great fish that must have weighed ten pounds each. It took the combined efforts of Friday and herself to land them.

I am convinced that, for bright color and strange markings, there are no fish in the world like those of Vao. Osa called them Impossible Fish. There were seldom two of the same color or shape in her day's catch. They were orange and red and green and silver, and sometimes varicolored. But the most noticeable were little blue fish about the size of sardines which went in schools of thousands through the still sea, coloring it with streaks of the most brilliant shimmering blue you can imagine. In addition to the Impossible Fish, there were many octopi, which measured about three feet from tentacle to tentacle, and there were shellfish by the thousand. On the opposite side of the island from that on which we lived, oysters grew on the roots of mangrove trees at the water's edge, and at low tide we used to walk along and pick them off as if they had been fruit.

We worked hard for the first week or so after our return to Vao, for we had about a hundred and fifty plates and nearly two hundred kodak films to develop. Previous to this trip, I had been forced to develop motion-picture films, as well as kodak films and plates, as I went along. Like most photographers, I had depended upon a formalin solution to harden the gelatin films and keep them from melting in the heat. Though such a solution aids in the preservation of the film, it interferes considerably with the quality of the picture, which often is harsh in outline as a result of the thickening of the film, and it is not a guarantee against mildew or against the "fogging" of negatives. Before starting for the New Hebrides, however, I had worked out a method of treating films that did not affect the quality of the picture, and yet made it possible to develop films successfully at a temperature much higher than 65°. Still better, it permitted me to seal my film after exposure and await a favorable opportunity for developing. Only lately I have developed in a New York workshop films that were exposed nineteen months ago in the New Hebrides and that were carried about for several months under the blaze of a tropical sun. They are among the best pictures I have ever taken.

Any one who has tried motion-picture photography in the tropics will realize what it means to be freed from the burden of developing all films on the spot. To work from three o'clock until sunrise, after a day of hard work in enervating heat, is usually sheer agony. Many a time I have gone through with the experience only to see the entire result of my work ruined by an accident. I have hung up a film to dry (in the humid atmosphere of the tropics drying often requires forty-eight hours instead of half as many minutes) and found it covered with tiny insects or bits of sand or pollen blown against it by the wind and embedded deep in the gelatin. I have covered it with mosquito-net in an effort to avoid a repetition of the tragedy and the mosquito-net has shut off the air and caused the gelatin to melt. I have had films mildew and thicken and cloud and spot, in spite of every effort to care for them. On this trip, though even so simple an operation as the changing of motion-picture film and the sealing of negatives was an arduous task when it had to be performed in cramped quarters, it was a great relief to be able to seal up my film and forget it after exposure. The plates that I used in my small camera had to be promptly attended to, however, for to have treated them as I treated the motion-picture film would have meant adding considerably to the bulk and weight of the equipment we were forced to carry about with us.

We worked at the developing several hours a day, and between times we explored the island, learning what we could of native life. Arree, the boy who acted as our maid-of-all-work, supplied me with native words until I had a fairly respectable vocabulary, but, when I tried to use it, I made the interesting discovery that the old men and the young men spoke different tongues. Language changes rapidly among savage tribes. No one troubles to get the correct pronunciation of a word. The younger generation adopt abbreviations or new words at will and incorporate into their speech strange corruptions of English or French words learned from the whites. Some of the words I learned from Arree were absolutely unintelligible to many of the older men. I found, too, that the language varied considerably from village to village, and though many of the Vao men were refugees from Malekula, it was very different from that of any of the tribes on the big island. I once estimated the number of languages spoken in the South Seas at four hundred. I am now convinced that as many as that are used by the black races alone.

As we poked about Vao, we decided that the island would be a good place in which to maroon the people who have the romantic illusion that savages lead a beautiful life. We had long ago lost that illusion, but even for us Vao had some surprises. One day, I made a picture of an old, blind man, so feeble that he could scarcely walk. He was one of the few really old savages about, and I gathered that he must have been a powerful chief in his day, or otherwise he would not have escaped the ordinary penalty of age—being buried alive. But on the day after I had taken his picture, when I went to his hut to speak to him, I was informed that "he stop along ground" and I was shown a small hut, in which was a freshly dug grave. My notice of the old man had drawn him into the limelight. The chiefs had held a conference and decided that he was a nuisance. A grave was dug for him, he was put into it, a flat stone was placed over his face so that he could breathe (!), and the hole was filled with earth. Now a devil-devil man was squatting near the grave to be on hand in case the old man asked for something. There was no conscious cruelty in the act, simply a relentless logic. The old man had outlived his usefulness. He was no good to himself or to the community. Therefore, he might as well "stop along ground."

Only a few days later, as we approached a village, we heard, at intervals, the long-drawn-out wail of a woman in pain. In the clearing we discovered a group of men laughing and jeering at something that was lying on the ground. That something was a writhing, screaming young girl. The cause of her agony was apparent. In the flesh back of her knee, two great holes had been burned. I could have put both hands in either of them.

"One fellow man, him name belong Nowdi, he ketchem plenty coconuts, he ketchem plenty pigs, he ketchem plenty Mary," said Arree, and he went on to explain that the "Mary" on the ground was the newest wife of Nowdi, whom he pointed out to us among the amused spectators. The savage had paid twenty pigs for her—a good price for a wife in the New Hebrides—but he had made a bad bargain; for the girl did not like him. Four times she ran away from him and was caught and brought back. The last time, nearly six months had elapsed before she was found, hiding in the jungle of the mainland. The day before we saw the girl, the men of the village had gathered in judgment. A stone was heated white-hot. Then four men held the girl while a fifth placed the stone in the hollow of her knee, drew her leg back until the heel touched the thigh, and bound it there. For an hour they watched her anguish as the stone slowly burned into her flesh. Then they turned her loose. Thenceforth she would always have to hobble, like an old woman, with the aid of a stick. She would never run away again.

We turned aside, half sick. It was hard for me to keep my hands off the brutes that stood laughing around the girl. Only the knowledge that to touch them would be suicide for me and death or worse for Osa held me back. But as we returned to the bungalow, I gradually cooled down. I realized that it was not quite fair to judge these savages—still in the stage of development passed by our own ancestors hundreds of thousands of years ago—according to the standards of civilized society. And I remembered how beastly even men of my own kind sometimes are when they are released from the restraints of civilization.

The next morning, after our morning swim, Osa and I sat on the beach and watched the commuters set off for Malekula. In some fifty canoes, "manned" by women, the entire female population went to the big island every day to gather firewood and fruit and vegetables. For the small island of Vao could not support its four hundred inhabitants, and the native women had accordingly made their gardens on the big island. This morning, as usual, the women were accompanied by an armed guard; for although the bush natives of Malekula were supposed to be friendly, the Vao men did not take any chances when it came to a question of losing their women. Late in the evening the canoes came back again. The women had worked all day, many of them with children strapped to their backs; the men had lounged on the beach, doing nothing. But it was the women who paddled the canoes home. There was a stiff sea and it took nearly three hours to paddle across the mile-wide channel. But the men never lifted a finger to help. When the boats were safely beached, the women shouldered their big bundles of vegetables and firewood and trudged wearily toward their villages, the men bringing up the rear, with nothing to carry except their precious guns. Among the poor female slaves— they were little more—we saw five who hobbled along with the aid of sticks. They were women who had tried to run away.

A few days later, Arree asked us if we should like to attend a feast that was being held to celebrate the completion of a devil-devil, one of the crude, carved logs that are the only visible signs of religion among the savages. We did not see why that should be an event worth celebrating, for there were already some hundreds of devil-devils on the island, but we were glad to have the opportunity of witnessing one of the feasts of which Arree had so often told us.

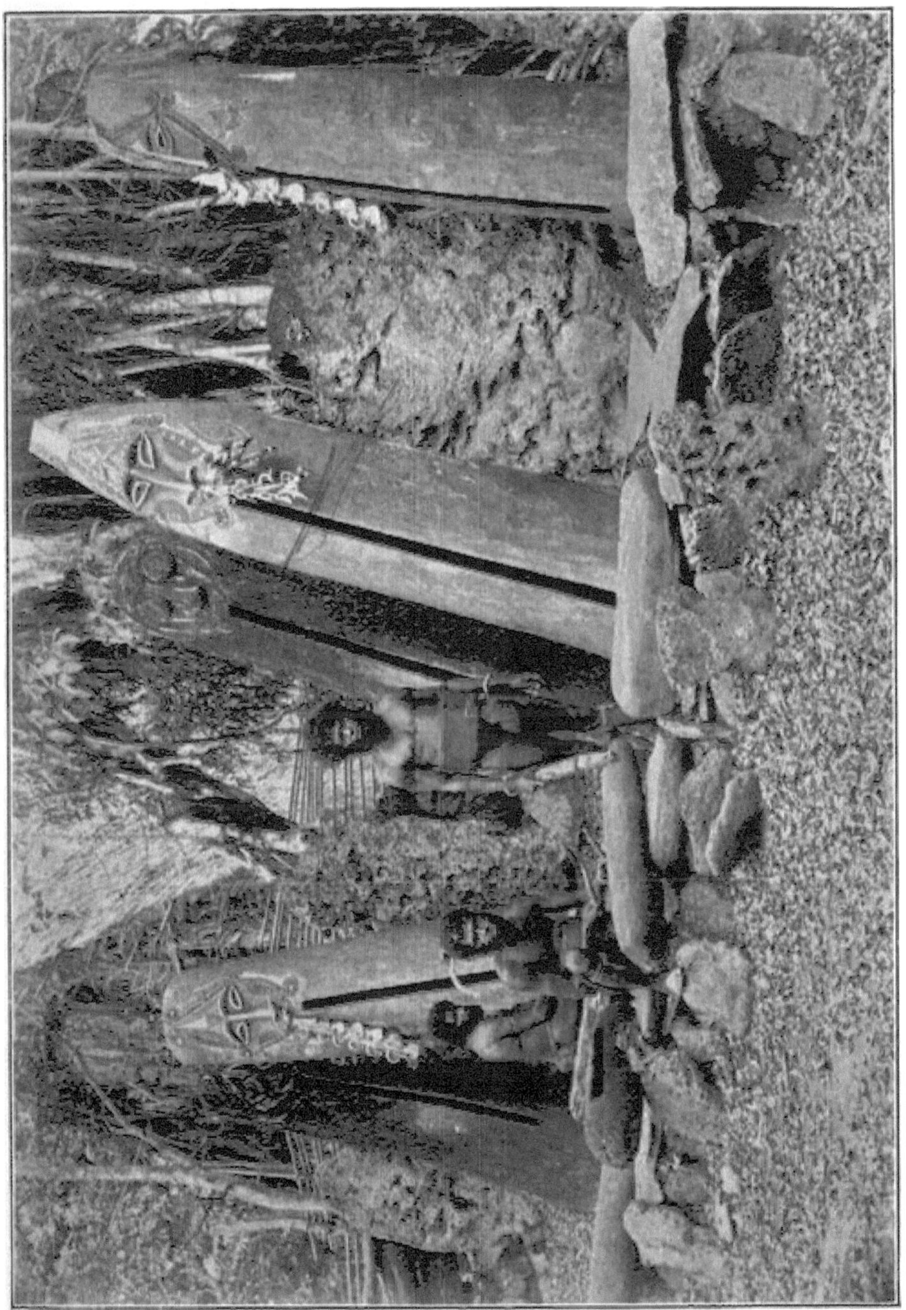

NAGAPATE AMONG THE DEVIL-DEVILS

Feasting was about the only amusement of the natives of Vao. A birth or a
death, the building of a house or a canoe, or the installation of a chief—any event

in the least out of the ordinary furnished an excuse for an orgy of pig meat—usually "long." The one we attended was typical. First the new devil-devil was carried into the clearing and, with scant ceremony, set up among the others. Then some of the men brought out about a hundred pigs and tied them to posts. Others piled hundreds of yams in the center of the clearing, and still others threw chickens, their legs tied together, in a squawking heap. When all was ready, the yams were divided among the older men, each of whom then untied a pig from a post and presented it solemnly to his neighbor, receiving in return another pig of about the same size. The savages broke one front and one hind leg of their pigs and threw the squealing little beasts on the ground beside the yams. Then they exchanged chickens and promptly broke the legs and wings of their fowls. I shall never forget the terrible crunching of bones and the screaming of the tortured pigs and chickens. When the exchange was completed, the men took their pigs to the center of the clearing, beat them over the head with sticks until they were nearly dead and threw them down to squeal and jerk their lives away.

When the exchange of food was completed, the men built little fires all around the clearing to cook the feast. Most of them were chiefs. It is a general rule throughout the region that no chief may eat food prepared by an inferior, or cooked over a fire built by an inferior. The rather doubtful honor of being his own cook is, indeed, practically the only mark that distinguishes a chief. As a rule a chief has no real authority. He cannot command the least important boy in his village. Only his wives are at his beck and call—and they are forbidden by custom to cook for him!

Chieftainship is an empty honor on Vao. If the biggest chief on the island should start off on a hunting trip and forget his knife, he would know better than to ask the poorest boy in the party to go back for it, for he would know in advance that the answer would be most emphatic Vao equivalent for "go chase yourself!" Yet a chieftaincy is sufficiently flattering to the vanity of the incumbent to be worth many pigs. The pig is more important in the New Hebrides than anywhere else in the world. A man's wealth is reckoned in pigs, and a woman's beauty is rated according to the number of pigs she will bring. The greatest chiefs on Vao are those who have killed the most pigs. Even in that remote region there is political corruption, for some men are not above buying pigs in secret to add to their "bag" and their prestige. Tethlong, who, during our stay on the island, was the most important chief on Vao, bought five hundred porkers to be slaughtered for the feast that made him chief. All the natives knew he had bought the pigs; but they hailed him solemnly, nevertheless, as the great pig-killer.

Tethlong had as fine a collection of pigs' tusks as I have ever seen. These fierce-looking bits of ivory did not come off the wild pigs, however, but were carefully cultivated on the snouts of domesticated pigs. It is the custom throughout the New Hebrides to take young pigs and gouge out two upper teeth, so as to make room for the lower canine teeth to develop into tusks. The most valuable tusks are those that have grown up and curled around so as to form two complete circles. These, however, are very rare. The New Hebridean native considers himself well off if he has a single circlet to wear as a bracelet or nose ring and he takes pride in a collection of ordinary, crescent-shaped tusks.

Pigs' tusks are the New Hebridean equivalent of money. For even among savages, there are rich and poor. The man of wealth is the one who has the largest number of pigs and wives and coconut trees and canoes, acquired by judicious swapping or by purchase, with pigs' tusks, rare, orange-colored cowries, and stones of strange shape or coloring as currency. Most natives keep such treasures in "bokkus belong bell"—a Western-made box with a bell that rings whenever the lid is lifted. But this burglar-alarm is utterly superfluous, for natives uncontaminated by civilization never steal.

Osa refused to watch the process of preparing the pigs and fowls for broiling. It was not a pretty sight. But it was speedily over. While the cooking was in progress, the dancing began. A group of men in the center of the clearing went through the motions of killing pigs and birds and men. Each tried to get across the footlights the idea that he was a great, strong man. And though the pantomime was crude, it was effective. The barbaric swing of the dancers, in time to the strange rhythm beaten out on the boo-boos—the hollowed logs that serve as drums—got into my blood, and I understood how the dances sometimes ended in an almost drunken frenzy.

When the first group of dancers were tired, the older men gathered in the center of the clearing and palavered excitedly. Then they retired to their fires and waited. So did we. But nothing happened save another dance. This was different in detail from the first. I never saw a native do exactly the same dance twice, though in essentials each is monotonously similar to the last. When the second dance was over, there was more palavering and then more dancing—and so on interminably. Osa and I grew sleepy and went back to the bungalow. But the tom-toms sounded until dawn.

CHAPTER VIII
GOOD-BYE TO NAGAPATE

The Euphrosyne, with the British Commissioner aboard, was about two weeks overdue and we were growing impatient to be off. It was not the Euphrosyne, however, but the queerest vessel I have ever seen, that anchored off Vao, one night at midnight. She was about the size of a large schooner and nearly as wide in the beam as she was long. She had auxiliary sails, schooner-rigged. Her engine burned wood. And her name—as we discovered later—was Amour. Queer as she was, she was a Godsend to us, marooned on Vao. We went out in a canoe and found, to our surprise, that the commander and owner was Captain Moran, whom we had met in the Solomons two years before. We asked him where he was bound for. He said that he had no particular destination; he was out to get copra wherever he could get it. I proposed that he turn over his ship to us at a daily rental, so that we could continue our search for signs of cannibalism among the tribes of Malekula. He assented readily. Osa and I were delighted, for we knew that there wasn't a better skipper than Captain Moran in the South Seas. Both he and his brother, who acted as engineer, were born in the islands and had spent their lives in wandering from one group to another. They knew the treacherous channels as well as any whites in those waters, and they knew the natives, too, from long experience as traders.

The next morning, while the crew of the schooner were cutting wood for fuel, we packed our supplies on board the Amour. When all was ready, we pulled up anchor, set the sails, and started the engine. After a few grunts, the propeller began to turn, and we were on our way.

Her ungainly shape served to make the Amour seaworthy, but it did not conduce to speed. We wheezed along at a rate of three knots an hour. Though we left Vao at dawn, it was nearly dark when we again reached Tanemarou Bay, the "seaport" of the Big Numbers territory. There was no one on the beach, but we discharged a stick of dynamite and rolled ourselves in our blankets, sure that there would be plenty of natives on hand to greet us next morning.

We slept soundly, in spite of the pigs that roamed the deck, and were awakened at daylight by cries. About a hundred savages had gathered on the beach. We lost no time in landing, but to our disappointment, Nagapate had not come down to greet us. Only Velle-Velle, the prime minister, was on hand, and he was in a difficult mood. He gave me to understand that I had slighted him, on my previous visit, in my distribution of presents. I soon averted his displeasure with plenty of tobacco and the strangest and most wonderful plaything he had ever had—a football. It was a sight for sore eyes to see that dignified old savage, who ordinarily was as pompous as any Western prime minister, kicking his football about the beach.

At about ten o'clock, I took a few boys and went inland to get some pictures. Osa wanted to accompany me, but I set my foot down on it. I knew there was no danger for myself, but I felt that Nagapate's interest in her made it unsafe for her to venture. I went to the top of a hill a few miles back, where I made some fine pictures of the surrounding country, and was lucky enough to get a group of savages coming over the ridge of another hill about half a mile away. My guides became panicky when they saw the newcomers, and insisted that we return to the beach at once, but I held firm until the last savage on the opposite hill had been lost to sight in the jungle. Then with enough film to justify my morning's climb, I returned to the beach.

On the following morning, Nagapate made his appearance, and told me, through Atree, that he had brought his wives to see Osa. I sent the boat to the schooner for her, but when she appeared, Nagapate said that his wives could not come to the beach and that Osa, accordingly, must go inland as far as the first river to meet them. I did not like the idea, but decided that no possible harm could come to her if the armed crew of the Amour and Captain Moran and I accompanied her. It turned out that my distrust of Nagapate was again unjustified. We found the wives waiting at the designated spot with sugar-cane and yams and a nice, new Big Numbers dress for Osa. They had not come to the beach because the newest wife was not permitted to look at the sea for a certain time after marriage—which seemed to me to carry the taboo on water a bit too far.

Osa was pleased to add the Big Numbers dress to her collection of strange things from Melanesia. And indeed it was quite a gift. For in spite of their apparent simplicity, the making and dyeing of the pandanus garments is a complicated process. Since the grass will not take the dye if it is the least green, it has to be dried and washed and dried again. When it is thoroughly bleached, it is dyed deep purple.

After Osa in turn had presented the wives with salmon and sea-biscuits (which I afterward saw Nagapate and his men devouring) and strings of bright-colored beads, Nagapate agreed to get his men to dance for me, if I would come to his village. I did not relish the idea of the long trip into the hills, but I wanted the picture. Osa returned to the schooner, and Captain Moran and I, with five boys, went inland. We made the village in four hours. When we arrived, I was ready to drop with exhaustion, and lay down on the ground for half an hour to recover. Savages squatted about me and watched me while I rested, then crowded about me while I got my cameras ready for action. Nagapate sent out for the men to come to the clearing, and they straggled in, sullen and cranky. They did not want to dance, but Nagapate's word was law. At his command, a few men went to the great boo-boos and beat out a weird rhythm that seemed to me to express the very essence of cannibalism. At first the savages danced in a half-hearted fashion, but gradually they warmed up. Soon they were doing a barbaric dance better than any I had ever seen. They marched quickly and in perfect time around the boo-boos. Then they stopped suddenly, with a great shout, stood for a moment marking time with their feet, marched on again and stopped again, and so on, the march becoming faster and faster and the shouting wilder and more continuous, until at last the dancers had to stop from sheer exhaustion.

I got a fine picture, well worth the long trip up the mountains, but it was very late before we got started beachward, accompanied by Nagapate and a number of his men. We went down the slippery trail as fast as we could go. I should have been afraid, in my first days in the islands, that the boys might fall with my cameras if we went at such a rate, but by now I had found that they were as sure-footed as mountain sheep. They carried my heavy equipment as if it had been bags of feathers and handled it much more carefully than I should have been able to.

In spite of our haste, it grew dark before we reached the beach. The boys cut dead bamboo for torches and in the uncertain light they gave, we stumbled along. When we were within about a quarter of a mile from the sea, we fired a volley to let Osa know that we were coming. To our surprise, when we came out on the beach, we were greeted by Osa and Engineer Moran and the remainder of the crew of the Amour, all armed to the teeth. Osa was crying. It was the first time I had ever known her to resort to tears in the face of danger. But when she learned that we were all there and safe, and that the volley had been a signal of our approach and not an indication that we had been attacked, her tears dried and she scolded me roundly for having frightened her.

I went to the boat and got a crate of biscuits and a small bag of rice and took them back to Nagapate for a feast for him and his men. Then I said good-bye. I believe that the old cannibal was really sorry to see us go—and not only for the sake of the presents we had given him. Some day I am going back to see him once more.

CHAPTER IX
THE MONKEY PEOPLE

At daylight we pulled anchor and set the sails and started the engine. With the wind to help us, we made good progress. In three hours we had reached our next anchorage, a small bay said to be the last frequented by the Big Numbers people. We were in the territory of the largest tribe on the west side of Malekula. Moran told me that no white man had ever penetrated the bush and that the people were very shy and wild. We landed, but saw no signs of savages. We thought we had the beach to ourselves, and I set about making pictures of a beautiful little river, all overhung with ferns and palms, that ran into the sea at one side of the bay. As I worked, one of the boys ran up to me and told me in very frightened *bêche-de-mer* that he had seen "plenty big fellow man along bush," and we beat a hasty retreat from the river, with its beautiful vegetation, well fitted for concealing savages.

I was very anxious to secure some photographs of the savages, and all the more so because they were said to be so difficult of approach, so I walked along the beach until I came to a trail leading into the interior. It was easy to locate the trail, for it was like a tunnel leading into the dark jungle. At its mouth, I set up my camera, attached a telephoto lens, bundled up a handful of tobacco in a piece of calico, placed my bait at the entrance of the trail, and waited. A half-hour passed, but nothing happened. Then, quick as a wink, a savage darted out, seized the bundle and disappeared before I had time to take hold of the crank of my camera. My trap had worked too well. Now I was determined to get results, so I had our armed crew withdraw to the edge of the beach and asked Captain Moran and Osa to set their guns against a rock so that the savages could see that we were not armed. I knew that, in case of emergency, we could use the pistols in our pockets. Then I sat down on my camera case and waited. At noon we sent one of the boys back to the boat for some tinned lunch. We ate with our eyes on the trail. It was two o'clock before four savages, with guns gripped tight in their hands, came cautiously out of the jungle, ready to run at the first alarm. I advanced slowly, so as not to frighten them, holding out a handful of tobacco and clay pipes. They timidly took my presents, and I tried to make them understand, by friendly gestures and soft words, which they did not comprehend, that we could not harm them. To make a long story short, I worked all afternoon to gain their confidence—and it was work wasted, for I could get no action from them. They simply stood like hitching-posts and let me take pictures all around them. At sundown we went back to the ship, with nothing to show for our day's effort.

Next morning, we set sail betimes. It did not take us long to reach Lambumba

Bay, on the narrow isthmus that connects northern and southern Malekula. I had been anxious to visit this region, for I had heard conflicting tales concerning it. Some said that it was inhabited by nomad tribes; others said that the nomads were a myth—that the region was uninhabited. I wanted to see for myself. So I instructed Captain Moran to find a good anchorage, where the ship would be sheltered in case a westerly wind should spring up. I wanted him to feel safe in leaving the Amour in charge of a couple of blacks, for I needed him and his brother and the majority of the crew to accompany us into the interior. We found a small cove at the mouth of a stream and with the kedge anchor we drew the Amour in until the branches of the trees hung over the decks. At high tide we pulled the bow of the schooner up into the sand. At low tide she was almost high and dry, and she was safe from any ordinary blow. Since this was not the hurricane season, no great storm was to be expected. In the evening, Osa made up the lunch-bags for the following day, and early next morning, we struck inland along a well-beaten trail. We followed this trail all day, but we saw no signs of natives. Next day we took a second trail, which crossed the first. Again we met no one. But we found baskets hanging from a banian and the embers of a fire, still alive under a blanket of ashes.

Though we were accomplishing nothing, we were having a very enjoyable time, for this was the most beautiful part of Malekula we had seen. The trails were well-beaten and for the most part followed small streams that cut an opening in the dense jungle to let the breeze through. Here, as elsewhere, we were surrounded by gay tropical birds, and in the trees hung lovely orchids. Osa kept the boys busy climbing after the flowers. They were plainly amazed at the whim of this white "Mary," who filled gasoline tins with useless flowers, but they obeyed her willingly enough, and she, with arms full of the delicate blossoms, declared that she was willing to spend a month looking for the savages.

We discovered them, however, sooner than that. On the third morning we took a new trail. We were walking along very slowly. I was in the lead. I turned a sharp corner around a big banian—and all but collided with a savage. The savage was as astonished as I, but he got his wits back more quickly than I did mine, and flitted off into the jungle as quietly as a butterfly. When the others came, I could scarcely make them believe that I had seen him; for he left no trail in the underbrush, and they had not heard a sound. In the hope of surprising other natives, we agreed to stay close together and to make as little noise as possible. In about half an hour four natives appeared on the brow of a low hill, directly in front of us. They, too, turned at the sight of us and ran off.

We followed along the trail by which they had disappeared. In about fifteen minutes we stopped to rest near a great banian. Now the banian, which is characteristic of this section of Malekula, begins as a parasite seedling that takes root in a palm or some other tree. This seedling grows and sends out branches, which drop ropelike tendrils to the ground. The tendrils take root and gradually thicken into trunks. The new trunks send out other branches, which in turn drop their tendrils, and so on, indefinitely. The banian near which we had stopped was some twenty feet in diameter. Its many trunks grew close together and it was covered with a crown of great heart-shaped leaves. Since conditions seemed favorable for a picture, I got a camera ready and turned to the tree to study the lights and shadows before I adjusted the shutters. As I grew accustomed to the light, I saw dimly, peering from behind the tendrils, four intent black faces. We had caught up with the men we had surprised on the trail.

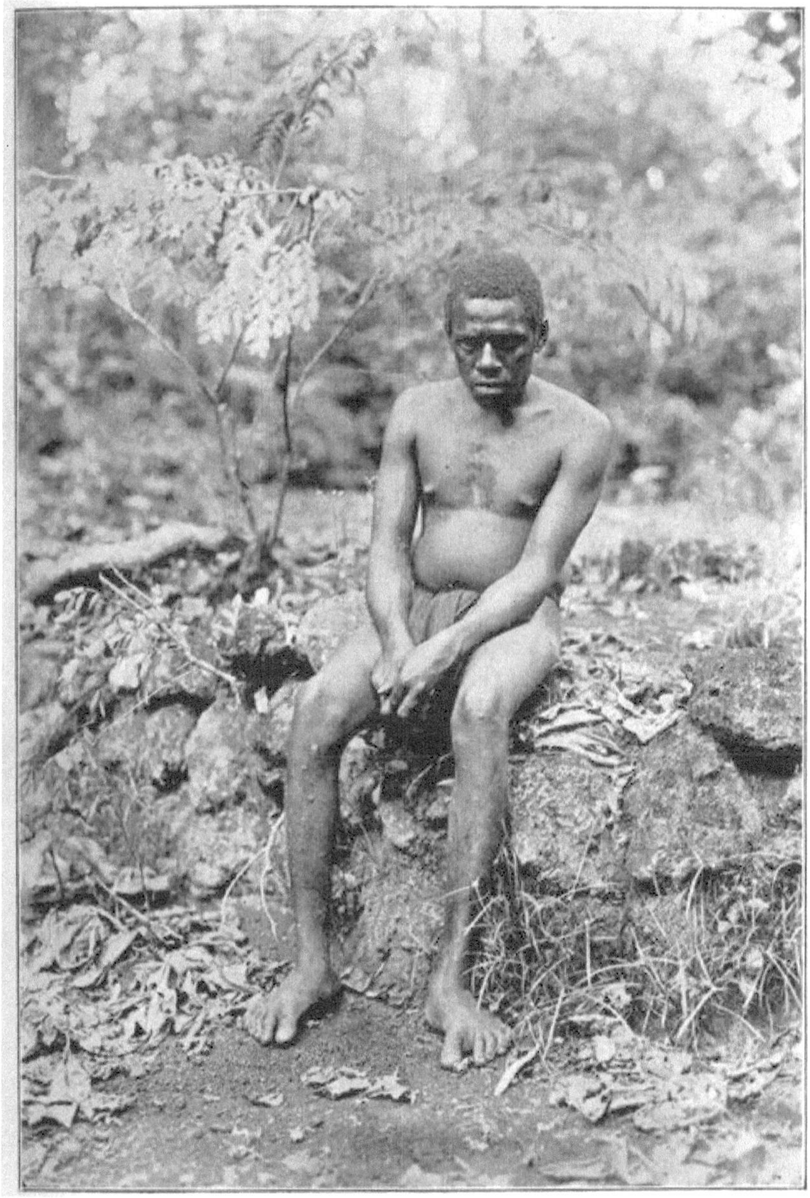

ONE OF THE MONKEY MEN

I spent an hour in trying to coax them into the open. I held out toward them the things most coveted by the natives of the New Hebrides — tobacco, salt, a knife, a piece of red calico. But they did not stir. I made an attractive heap of presents on the ground and we all stood back, hoping that the shy savages would pick up courage to come out and examine them. But they refused to be tempted. At last I lost patience and ordered the boys to surround the banian. When I was sure that we had the natives cornered, I went under the tree and hunted around among its many trunks for my captives. There was not a sign of them. But in the center of the banian was an opening in which hung long ladders fashioned from the tendrils. The savages had escaped over the tops of the trees. We did not get another glimpse of them that day, but when we returned to the Amour, we saw footprints in the sand of the beach. And the two boys we had left in charge said that a number of savages had inspected the vessel from a distance, disappearing into the jungle just before our arrival.

I was convinced by this time that we had really discovered the nomads, but I began to despair of ever getting a close-up of them. Early next morning, however, as we were eating breakfast, a native who might have been twin brother to those of the banian marched boldly down the beach and up to the side of the ship. In bad *bêche-de-mer* he asked us who we were and where we came from and what we wanted. We learned that he had been "blackbirded" off to Queensland long before and had made his way back home after a year's absence. He knew all about the white men and their ways, he told us, and proved it by asking for tobacco.

I gladly got out some tobacco and gave it to him. Then he informed us that he had no pipe and I made him happy with a clay pipe and a box of matches.

I invited him to come on board, but he refused; one "blackbirding" experience had been enough for him. He squatted on the sand, within talking distance, and told us what a great man he was. He was the only one of his tribe who knew "talk belong white man." He was a famous fighter. The enemies of his people ran when they saw him. He had killed many men and many pigs. He recited his virtues over and over, utterly ignoring my questions about his people. But finally I succeeded in extracting from him an agreement to guide us to the headquarters of his tribe.

When we stood on the shore, ready to go, Nella—for that was the name of our visitor—looked Osa over from head to foot. She wore her usual jungle costume of khaki breeches and high boots. When he had completed his inspection, he turned to me and said wisely, "Me savvy. He Mary belong you." Then, adding in a business-like tone, "Me think more better you bringem altogether tobacco," he turned and led the way into the jungle.

He took us along one of the trails that we had followed in vain during the preceding days. But presently he turned off into another trail that we had not noticed. The entrance was masked with cane-grass. After about ten feet, however, the path was clean and well-beaten. When we had passed through the cane, Nella returned and carefully straightened out the stalks that we had trampled down.

When we had traversed a mile or so of trail, Nella called a halt and disappeared into the depths of a banian. Soon he returned, followed by three young savages and an old man, who was nearer to a monkey than any human being I have ever seen before or since—bright eyes peering out from a shock of woolly hair; an enormous mouth disclosing teeth as white and perfect as those of a dental advertisement; skin creased with deep wrinkles; an alert, nervous, monkey-like expression; quick, sure, monkey-like movements. He approached us carefully, ready to turn and run at the slightest alarm. I endeavored to shake hands with him, but he jerked his hand away. The friendly greeting had no meaning for him. My presents, however, talked to him. Reassured by them and the voluble Nella, who was greatly enjoying his position as master of ceremonies, the savages squatted near us.

I began digging after information, but information was hard to get. Nella preferred asking questions to answering them. All that I could learn from him was that there were many savages in the vicinity and that we would see them all in due time.

The conversation became one-sided. The five savages sat and discussed us in their own language of growls and ape-like chattering. They tried to examine the rifles carried by our boys, but the boys were afraid to let their guns out of their hands. Osa, more confident, explained to the savages the working of her repeater. Then they focused their attention on her. They felt her boots and grunted admiringly. They fingered her blond hair and carefully touched her skin, giving strange little whistles of awe. Osa was used to such attentions from savages and took them as a matter of course.

In spite of their grotesque appearance, there was little that was terrifying about our new acquaintances. They seemed not at all warlike. Only two of the five carried weapons, the one a bow and arrow, the other a club. I was interested to observe that the old man, who apparently was a chief, wore the Big Numbers costume—a great clout of pandanus fiber—while the others were still more lightly clothed according to the style in vogue among the Small Numbers. I tried to find out the reason for the variation. But Nella was not interested in my questions. Finally, I realized that there was no use in trying to get information in a hurry. Time means nothing to savages. We examined the banian from which our visitors had come. Like the tree we had seen on the previous day, it had a hole in the center, in which hung a ladder for hasty exits. Empty baskets, hung from the branches, showed that the place was much frequented.

After a while about twenty natives came along the trail. They joined the five natives already with us, and the examination of us and our belongings began all over. Osa went among the newcomers with her kodak, taking snapshots, and I set up my moving-picture camera on a tripod, selected a place where the light was good, and tried to get the savages in front of my lens. They would not move; so I pointed my camera at them and began to turn the crank. Like lightning, they sprang to their feet and ran to the banian. They scampered up the tendrils like monkeys, and by the time I could follow them with the camera, I could see only their bright eyes here and there peering from the crevices.

Through Nella we coaxed them back, and down they came, as quickly as they had gone up, while I ground out one of the best pictures I ever got. Osa at once dubbed them the "monkey people." And indeed they were nearer monkeys than men. They had enormous flat feet, with the great toe separated from the other toes and turned in. They could grasp a branch with their feet as easily as I could with my hands. For speed and sureness and grace in climbing, they outdid any other men I had ever seen.

When luncheon-time came, we spread out our meal of cold broiled wood-pigeon, tinned asparagus, and sea-biscuit and began to eat. After watching us for a few moments, two or three savages went and fetched some small almond-like nuts, which they shared with their companions. They seemed more like monkeys than ever as they squatted there, busily cracking the nuts with stones and picking out the meats with their skinny fingers.

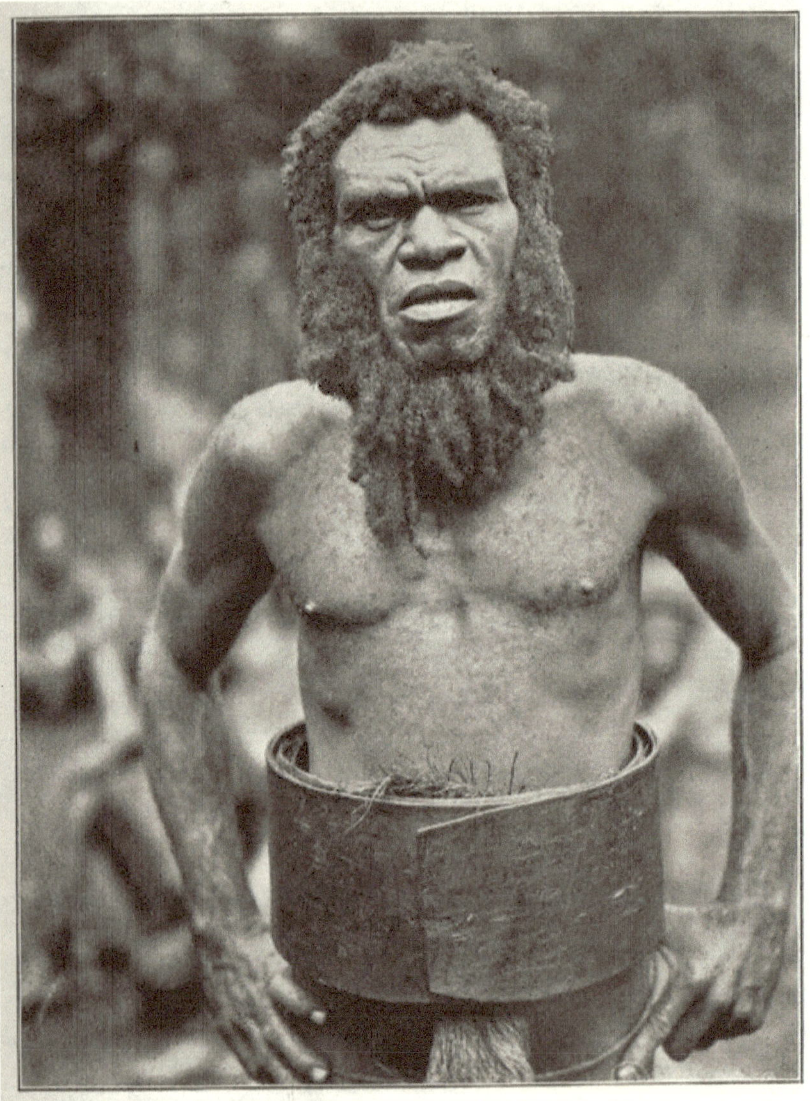

WO-BANG-AN-AR

By dint of many presents, I won the confidence of the chief and, before the afternoon was over, I was calling him by his first and only name, which was, as near as I can spell it phonetically, Wo-bang-an-ar. He was a strange crony. He was covered with layer after layer of dirt. No one who has not been among savage tribes can image a human being so filthy. His hair had never been combed or cut; it was matted with dirt and grease. His eyes were protruding and bloodshot and they were never still. His glance darted from one to another of us and back again. But, like Nagapate, he proved to be a real chief, and his people jumped whenever he gave a command. He ordered them to do whatever I asked, and I made pictures all the afternoon.

That night we slept in the banian, and next day Nella led us through the jungle to a clearing some five miles distant. There we found about a hundred men, women, and children. All of them, save Wo-bang-an-ar, who had his food supplied to him by his subjects, looked thin and drawn. Some of the men wore the Big Numbers costume, some that of the Small Numbers. The women wore the usual Small Numbers dress of a few leaves. A few men carried old rifles, but they had only about half a dozen cartridges among them; a few others had bows and arrows or clubs, but the majority were unarmed. This seemed strange, in the light of our experience among the tribes of northern Malekula, but even stranger was the fact that these people had no houses or huts—no dwellings of any kind. They lived in the banians. Sometimes they put a few leaves over the protruding roots as a shelter from rain. Occasionally, they built against the great central trunk of the tree a rough lean-to of sticks and leaves. Beyond that they made no attempt at constructing houses.

During the three days we spent among them, I picked up fragments of their history, which runs somewhat as follows:

Years ago, before the white men came to Malekula, there were many more people on the island than there are to-day. In the north and in the south there were great tribes, who were fierce and warlike. They fell upon the people who dwelt in the isthmus, and destroyed their villages. Again and again this happened. The tribes that lived in the isthmus grew smaller and smaller. Their men were killed and their women were carried off. Finally the few that were left no longer dared to build villages; for a village served merely to advertise their whereabouts to their enemies. They became nomads, living in trees. They even ceased the cultivation of gardens and depended for their food on wild fruits and nuts, the roots of trees, and an occasional bit of fish. Their number was augmented from time to time by refugees from the Big Numbers tribes on the north and from the Small Numbers on the south—a fact that explained the variation in dress we had noticed. They were unarmed, because their best means of defense was flight. They could not stand against their warlike neighbors, but they could elude them by climbing trees and losing themselves in the dark, impenetrable jungles.

CHAPTER X

THE DANCE OF THE PAINTED SAVAGES

After three days among the nomads, we decided that there was no cannibalism among a people so mild and spiritless, and so we packed our belongings and set off for the Amour. We thought we had half a day's journey ahead of us, but to our surprise we reached the ship in less than two hours. Nella, to be on the safe side, had led us to the headquarters of the tribe by a circuitous route.

It was high tide when we reached the beach; so we took the opportunity of getting the Amour off the sand. A good breeze took us rapidly down the coast. At nightfall we started the engine and by midnight we had anchored in Southwest Bay.

The next morning, at daybreak, we were surrounded by natives in canoes, with fruit and yams and fish for sale. Since the fish were old and smelly, we decided to catch some fresh ones by the dynamite method in use throughout the South Seas wherever there are white men to employ their "magic"! We lowered the two whaleboats. I set my camera in one and lashed the other alongside to steady my boat which bobbed about a good bit as it was, but not enough to spoil the picture. I next set the natives to hunting for a school of fish. In a few moments they signaled that they had found one. We approached slowly and quietly and threw the dynamite. It exploded with a roar and sent a spout of water several feet into the air. After the water had quieted, the fish began to appear. Soon some three hundred mullets, killed from the concussion, were floating on the surface and the natives jumped overboard and began to gather the fish into their canoes. Suddenly one of the blacks yelled in terror. He scrambled into his canoe and his companions did likewise. I saw the dark edge of a shark's fin coming through the water. He was an enormous shark and in his wake came a dozen others. They made the water boil as they gobbled down our catch. Captain Moran seized his gun and put a bullet through the nose of one of the largest of them. The shark leaped ten feet out of the water, and in huge jumps made for the open sea, lashing the water into foam with his tail every time he touched the surface. I got some fine pictures.

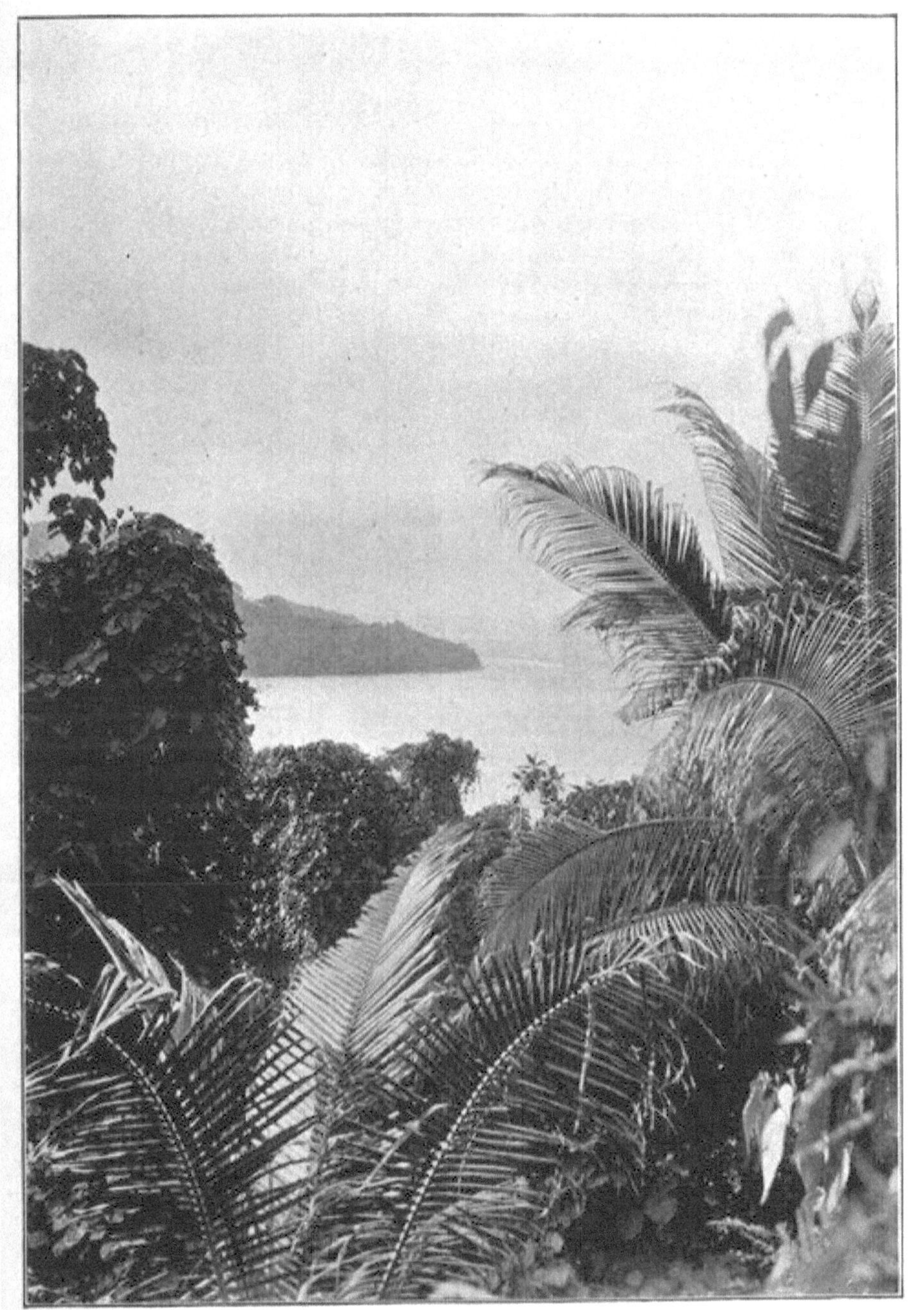

SOUTHWEST BAY

Before the sun was up, we were well on our way, with an escort of a dozen canoes. The river was broad and beautiful. On one side was a sandy beach. On the other was jungle, clear to the water's edge. After we had paddled for about two miles, we came unexpectedly into a lagoon about three miles long and two wide, and dotted with tiny, jungled islands. As we were making pictures of the lovely scene, several natives came out in canoes and invited us to land. They were the first of the long-headed people that we had seen. Their heads were about half as long again as they should have been and sloped off to a rounded point. We landed and visited several villages, each consisting of no more than three or four tumble-down huts. There were a few wretched, naked women, a half-dozen skinny children, and several half-starved pigs about. Some of the women had strapped to their backs babies who wore the strange baskets that mould their heads into the fashionable shape. One of these baskets is put on the head of each child when it is about three days old. First a cloth woven from human hair is fitted over the head. This is soaked with coconut oil to soften the skull. Then, after a few days, the basket is put on, and the soft skull immediately takes on the elongated shape desired. The basket is woven of coconut fiber in such a manner that the strands can be tightened day after day, until the bones are too hard to be further compressed. When the child is a year old, the basket is taken off.

In time gone by, the lagoon tribes, like the "monkey people," had suffered much from wars. The few survivors had lost interest in life. They no longer repaired their houses. Their devil-devils were falling into decay. The clearings, instead of being beaten hard, as is usually the case, were overgrown with grass; for dances and ceremonies were rare among these sadly disheartened folk.

Inside the houses were gruesome ornaments. Human heads, dried and smoked, hung from the rafters or leered from the ends of the poles on which they were impaled. In some houses there were mummified bodies, with pigs' tusks in the place of feet. Somehow, in the general atmosphere of decay, these things seemed pitiful rather than terrifying.

When we returned to the beach, a little after dark, the boys told us that scores of natives, well armed and painted in war-colors, had spent a day on the beach on the opposite side of the bay. As soon as it was daylight, we embarked in the whaleboat to look for them. For about five miles, we ran along the coast without seeing a trace of a human being. The jungle came down to the water's edge and dangled its vines in the water. But at last we came to a long, sandy beach well packed down by bare feet. A number of baskets hung from the trees at the edge of the jungle. We headed the boat for the shore, but just before she ran her nose into the sand, some twenty savages emerged without warning from the bush. One glance, and our boys frantically put out to sea again. We were thankful enough for their presence of mind, for the natives were a terrifying sight. Their faces and heads were striped with white lime; their black bodies were dotted with spots of red, yellow, blue, and white, and their bushy hair bristled with feathers. They all carried guns. How many of them had bullets was another question—but we did not care to experiment to find the answer.

When we were about fifty feet from shore, I called a halt and tried to get into communication with the natives. I had small success. They kept saying something over and over, but what it was, I could not understand. The tide carried us up the coast and the men followed at the water's edge. Finally, realizing that we did not trust them, they went back to the jungle and leaned their guns against a tree. Then they came down to the water-line again, and we rowed inshore until the bow of our boat was anchored in the sand.

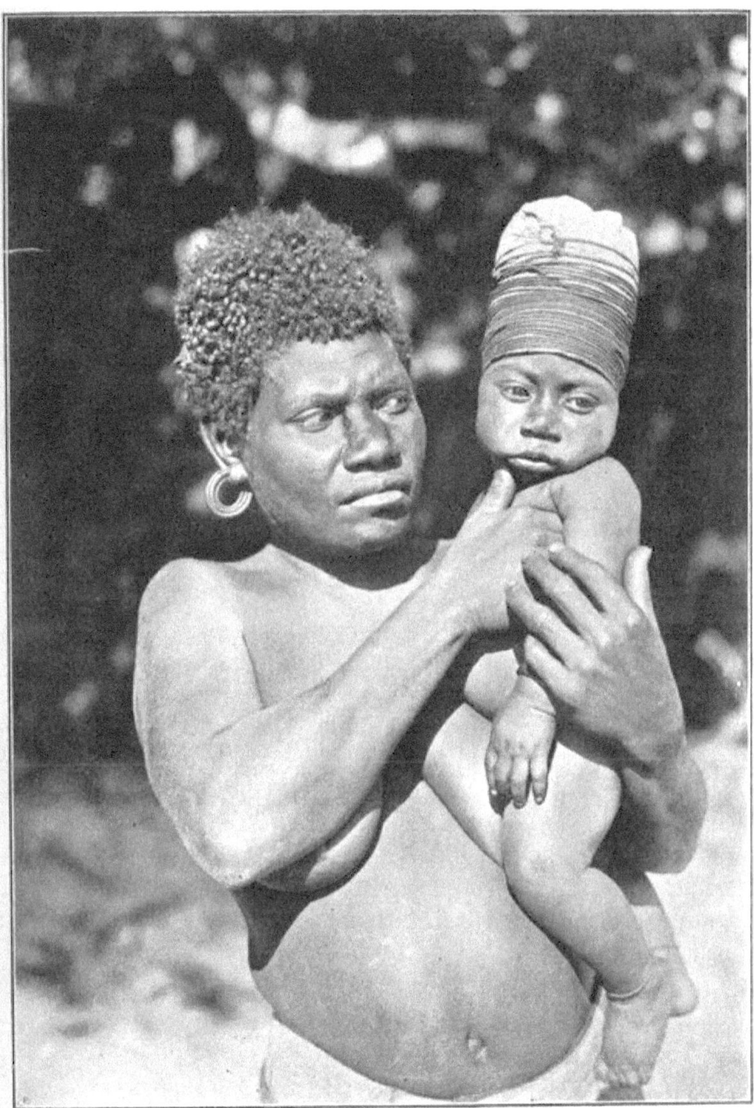

WOMAN AND CHILD OF THE LONG-HEADS, TOMMAN

The savages waded out to us. Our boys held their guns ready for action; for the visitors were certainly a nasty-looking lot. They were as naked as when they were born, and they had great, slobbery mouths that seemed to bespeak many a cannibal feast. They begged for tobacco and I gave each of them a stick and a clay pipe. Then one of them, who spoke a little *bêche-de-mer*, told us that a big feast was taking place at a village about three miles inland. He and his companions were waiting for the boo-boos to announce that it was time for them to put in an appearance.

I decided, and Captain Moran and his brother agreed with me, that there would be no danger in attending the ceremony. From what I could extract from the natives, I gathered that there would not be more than a hundred and fifty persons present. Our black boys seemed willing to make the trip—a good sign, for they were quick to scent danger and determined in avoiding it, so we landed.

Experience had taught me that the possession of a rifle does not necessarily make a native dangerous, and, sure enough, when I examined the guns leaning against the tree, I found that only four of the guns had cartridges. The rest were all too old and rusty to shoot.

Twenty savages led us inland over a good trail. Before we had walked half an hour, we could hear the boom of the boo-boos. I have never been able to get used to that sound. Often as I have heard it, it sends a chill down my spine. After an hour, it began to get on my nerves. By that time we had reached the foot of a steep hill, and our escort told us that they could go no farther until they were summoned. We went on alone, the sound of the boo-boos growing louder and more terrifying with each step. Osa began to wonder about the advisability of bursting on the natives unannounced. She hinted vaguely that it might be wise to return to the boat. But we kept on.

It was a hard climb. We had to stop several times to rest. The revolvers that Osa and I carried in our hip pockets seemed heavy as lead. At last, however, we made the top of the hill, and found ourselves at the edge of a clearing about a quarter of a mile in diameter. In the center, around a collection of huge boo-boos and devil-devils, were a thousand naked savages. That was my first estimate. A little later I divided the number in two, but even at that, there were more savages than I had ever before seen at one time. And they were the fiercest-looking lot I had ever laid my eyes on. White lead, calcimine, red paint, and common bluing are among the most valued trade articles in this region, and the savages had invested heavily in them, and besides had added to their make-up boxes yellow ocher and coral lime and ghastly purple ashes. Every single one had a gun or a bow and arrows, and looked as if he would use it at very slight provocation.

As we appeared, the boom of the boo-boos ceased. The savages who had been dancing stopped. Every eye was turned on us. After a moment's silence, all the natives began to talk. Then a number separated themselves from the mob, and, led by an old man who was smeared with yellow ocher from the crown of his head to the soles of his feet, approached us.

The old man spoke to us severely in *bêche-de-mer*, asking our business.

"We walk about, no more," I explained humbly. "We bringem presents for big fellow master belong village."

The haughty old man then informed us that, though he himself was the biggest chief of all, there were many other chiefs present, and that I must make presents to all of them. He was not at all polite about it. He said "must" and he meant "must." I took one glance at the hundreds of fierce, painted faces in the clearing, and then I had one of the boys bring me the big ditty-bag. Then and there I distributed about twenty-five dollars' worth of trade-stuff—the most I had ever given at one time.

The uproar was fairly deafening—I was thoroughly alarmed. The voices of the savages were angry. Men ran from group to group, apparently giving commands. Moran put his two hands in his pockets where he kept his revolvers and I told Osa to do likewise. Our boys huddled close around us. No need to tell them to keep their guns ready.

The bag was soon empty, and there was nothing further to do but await developments. To retreat would be more dangerous than to stay. In order to keep Osa from guessing how scared I was, I got out my moving-picture camera. I wish I could have photographed what happened then; for the entire mob broke and ran for cover. I wondered if they had ever seen a machine-gun. I couldn't explain their fright on any other grounds. Only old Yellow Ocher stood his ground. He was scared, but game, and asked me excitedly what I was up to. I explained the camera to him and opened it up and showed him the film and the wheels. He shouted to the other natives to come back, and they returned to the clearing, muttering and casting sullen glances in our direction. The old man was angry. We had nearly broken up the show. He gave us to understand that he washed his hands of us.

He then turned his attention to the ceremony. In a few moments a dozen savages took their places at the boo-boos and a few men started a half-hearted chant. A score of young savages began to dance, but without much spirit. It was half an hour before they warmed up, but at the end of that time the chant was loud and punctuated with blood-thirsty yells, and a hundred men were dancing in the clearing. I call the performance "dancing," but it was simply a march, round and round, quickening gradually to a run punctuated by leaps and yells. Soon women and children came out of the jungle. That was a good sign. For the time being, we were in no danger.

The dance ended abruptly with a mighty yell. The men at the boo-boos changed their rhythm and the twenty savages we had met on the beach burst from the jungle into the clearing and began to dance. There was a rough symbolism in their dance. But we could not decipher the meaning of the pantomime. They picked up a bunch of leaves here and deposited them there. Then they charged a little bundle of sticks and finally gathered them up and carried them off. When they were tired out, they withdrew to the side-lines, and another group, all painted alike, in an even fiercer pattern than that of the first group, made a similar dramatic entrance and danced themselves into exhaustion. They were followed by other groups. By the time three hours had passed, there were fully a thousand savages in the clearing.

It was a wonderful sight. My "movie" sense completely overcame my fears, and I ground out roll after roll of film. When the afternoon was well advanced, a hundred savages began to march to slow time around the devil-devils. Others joined in. They increased their pace. Soon more than half the natives were in a great circle, running and leaping and shouting around the clearing. Those who were left formed little circles of their own, the younger men dancing and the older ones watching with unfriendly eyes the actions of the rival groups. Even the women and children were hopping up and down and shouting. Occasionally a detachment of natives came toward us. At times we were completely surrounded, though we tried our best by moving backward to prevent the savages from getting in our rear.

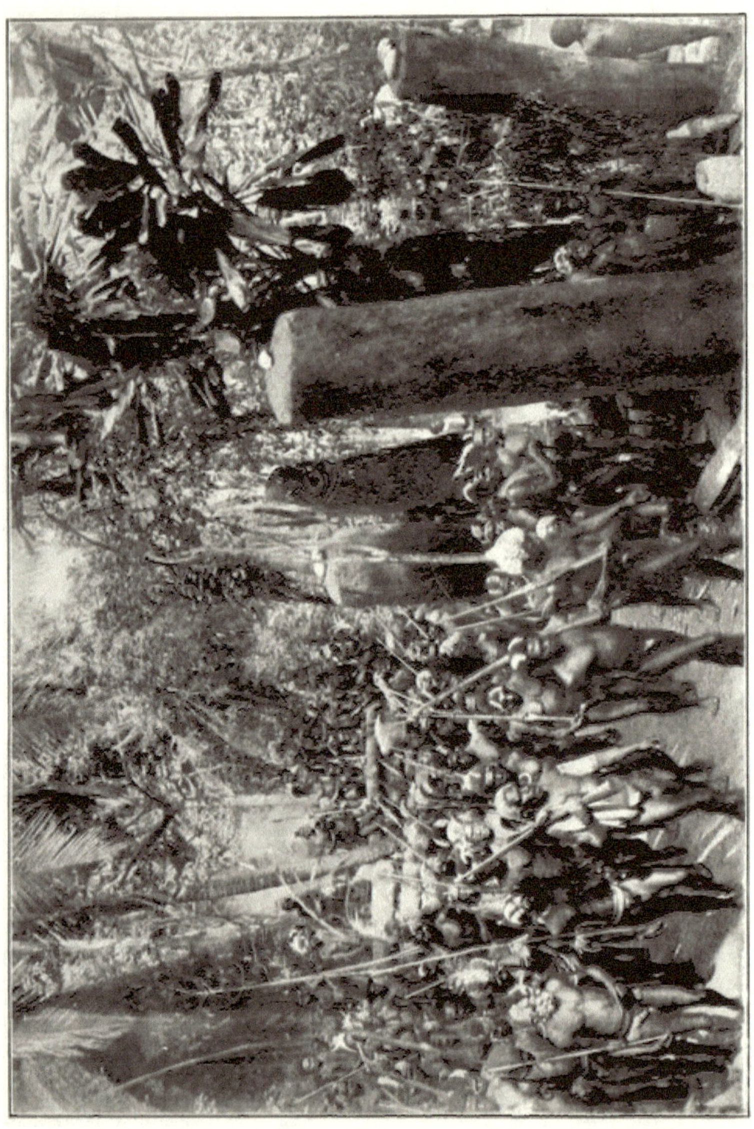

THE PAINTED DANCERS OF SOUTHWEST BAY

As the dance grew wilder, however, the savages lost all interest in us. Soon every one of them was dancing in the clearing. I shall never forget that dance—a thousand naked, painted savages, running and leaping in perfect time to the strange beat-beat-beat of the boo-boos and the wild, monotonous chant punctuated with brutal yells. The contagion spread to the women and children and they hopped up and down like jumping-jacks and chanted with the men. I turned the crank of my camera like mad. The sun sank behind the trees and Osa and Moran urged me to return to the beach, but I was crazy with excitement over the picture I was getting and I insisted on staying: I lighted a number of radium flares. The savages muttered a bit, but they were worked up to too high a pitch to stop the dance, and, when they found that the flares did no harm, they rather liked them. Old Yellow Ocher, seeing that the bluish-white light added to the spectacular effect, asked me for some more flares. I gave him my last two, and he put them among the devil-devils and lighted them. He could not have done me a greater service. The light from the flares made it possible to get a picture such as I never could have secured in the waning daylight.

The savages were sweating and panting with their exertions, but now they danced faster than ever. They seemed to have lost their senses. They leaped and shouted like madmen. Osa swallowed her pride and begged me to put up my camera, and at last I reluctantly consented. As I packed my equipment, I found two hundred sticks of tobacco that had escaped my notice. Without thinking of consequences, I put them on the edge of the clearing and motioned to Yellow Ocher to come and get them. But some of the young bucks saw them first. They leaped toward them. The first dozen got them. The next hundred fought for them. The dance ended in uproar.

For the first time in our island experiences, Osa was frightened. She took to her heels and ran as she had never run before. The boys grabbed up my cameras and followed her. Captain Moran stood by me. He urged me to run, but I felt that, if we did so, we should have the whole pack on us. Old Yellow Ocher and some of the other chiefs came up to us and yelled something that we could not understand and did not attempt to answer. There was no chance for explanations in that uproar. We edged toward the trail. The chiefs pressed after us, yelling louder than ever. Their men were at their heels. Luckily some of the natives began to fight among themselves and diverted the attention of the majority from us. Only a small group followed us to the edge of the hill. When we reached the trail, Moran said we had better cut and run, and we made the steep descent in record time.

Our boys were a hundred yards ahead of us. Osa, with nothing to carry, was far in the lead. When I caught up with her, she was crying, not with fear, but with anger. When she got her breath back, she told me what she thought of me for exposing us all to danger for the sake of a few feet of film. I took the scolding meekly, for I knew she was right. But I kept wishing that we had been twelve white men instead of three. Then I could have seen the dance through to the end.

CHAPTER XI

TOMMAN AND THE HEAD-CURING ART

We were safe on board the Amour, but we could still hear the boo-boos marking the time for the wild dance back in the hills. I awoke several times during the night. The boom-boom still floated across the water. I was glad that we had taken to our heels when we did, though I still regretted the picture I might have got if we could have stayed. At dawn, there was silence. The dance was over.

A trader who put in at Southwest Bay late in the morning told us of a man who had been brutally murdered at the very village we had visited. It was his belief that we had escaped only because the memory of the punitive expedition that had avenged the murder was still fresh in the minds of the natives. Even that memory might have failed to protect us, he told us, if the natives had really been in the heat of the dance. And he and Captain Moran swapped yarns about savage orgies until Osa became angry with me all over again for having stayed so long on the hill to witness the dance.

After a day's rest, we continued on our journey in search of cannibals. Our next stop was Tomman, an island about half a mile off the southernmost tip of Malekula. Since we found the shore lined with canoes, we expected to be surrounded as usual, as soon as we had dropped anchor, by natives anxious to trade. To our surprise, there was not a sign of life. We waited until it was dark and then gave up expecting visitors, for the savages of the New Hebrides rarely show themselves outside their huts after dark for fear of spirits. Early next morning, however, we were awakened by hoarse shouts, and found the Amour surrounded by native craft. We then discovered that we had arrived inopportunely in the midst of a dance. Dances in the New Hebrides are not merely social affairs. They all have some ceremonial significance and accordingly are not to be lightly interrupted.

Captain Moran assured us that, since the natives of this island, like those of Vao, were sufficiently acquainted with the Government gunboat to be on their good behavior where white men were concerned, it would be safe to go ashore. We launched a whaleboat and set out for the beach, escorted by about a hundred savages, who came to meet us in canoes. These natives, like some of those we had met with in the region around Southwest Bay, had curiously shaped heads. Their craniums were almost twice as long as the normal cranium and sloped to a point at the crown. The children, since their hair was not yet thick enough to conceal the conformation, seemed like gnomes with high brows and heads too big for their bodies.

When we reached shore, we beached the whaleboat at a favorable spot and, leaving it in charge of a couple of the crew, followed a well-beaten trail that led from the beach to a village near by. At the edge of a clearing surrounded by ramshackle huts, we stopped to reconnoiter.

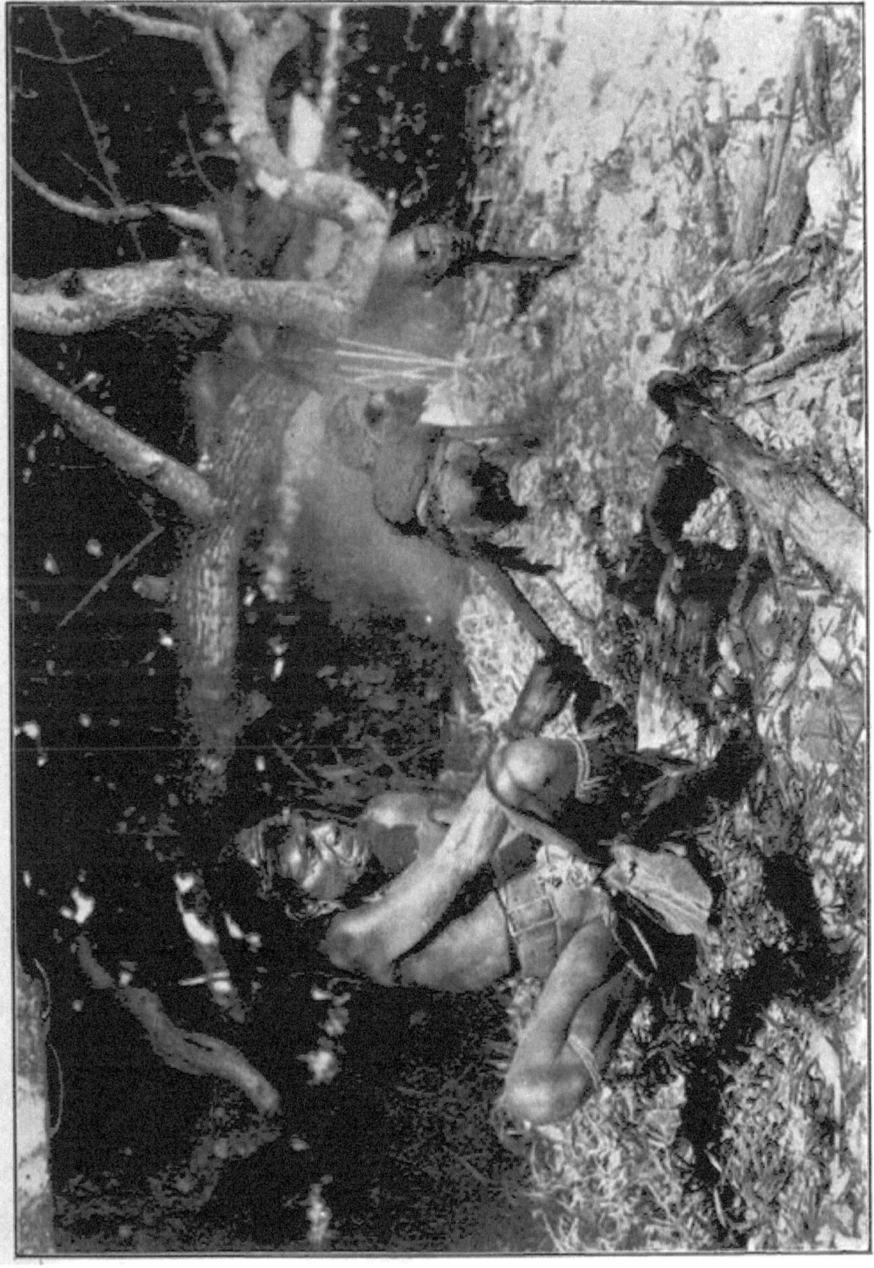

THE OLD HEAD-CURER

I have never seen a more eerie spectacle. In the center of the clearing, before a devil-devil, an old man was dancing. Very slowly he lifted one foot and very slowly put it down; then he lifted the other foot and put it down, chanting all the while in a hoarse whisper. At the farther side of the clearing, a group of old savages were squatting near a smoldering fire, intently watching one of their number, the oldest and most wizened of them all, as he held in the smoke a human head, impaled on a stick. Near by, on stakes set in the ground, were other heads.

The natives who had accompanied us up the trail shouted something and the men about the fire looked up. They seemed not at all concerned over our sudden appearance and made no attempt to conceal the heads. As for the old dancer, he did not so much as glance our way.

We went over to the men crouched about the fire and spoke to them. They paid scant attention to Moran and me, but they forsook their heads to look at Osa. She was always a source of wonder and astonishment to the natives, most of whom had never before seen a white woman. These old men went through the usual routine of staring at her and cautiously touching her hands and hair, to see if they were as soft as they appeared to be.

I discovered that the old head-curer knew *bêche-de-mer* and could tell me something of the complicated process of his trade. The head was first soaked in a chemical mixture that hardened the skin and, to a certain extent, at least, made it fireproof. Next, the curer held it over a fire, turning and turning it in the smoke until the fat was rendered out and the remaining tissue was thoroughly dried. After the head had been smeared with clay to keep it from burning, it was again baked for some hours. This process consumed about a week of constant work. The dried head was then hung up for a time in a basket of pandanus fiber, made in the shape of a circular native hut with a thatched roof, and finally it was exhibited in the owner's hut or in a ceremonial house; but for a year it had to be taken out at intervals and smoked again in order to preserve it.

The old head-curer was an artist, with an artist's pride in his work. He told me that he was the only one left among his people who really understood the complicated process of drying heads. The young men were forsaking the ways of their fathers. Of the old men, he was the most skilled. All the important heads were brought to him for curing, and he was employed to dry the bodies of great chiefs, smearing the joints with clay to keep the members from falling apart, turning each rigid corpse in the smoke of a smoldering fire until it was a shriveled mummy, painting the shrunken limbs in gay colors, and substituting pigs' tusks for the feet. The old man told me that heads nowadays are not what they were in olden times. He said what I found hard to believe—that the craniums of his ancestors were twice as long as those of present-day islanders.

Specimens of the head-curer's art were displayed in every hut in the village. The people of Tomman are not head-hunters in the strict sense of the word. They do not go on head-raids as do the men of Borneo. But if they kill an enemy, they take his head and hang it up at home to frighten off the evil spirits. The heads of enemies are roughly covered with clay and hastily and carelessly cured, but those of relatives are more scientifically treated, for they are to be cherished in the family portrait gallery. While the natives of Tomman do not produce works of art comparable to the heads treated by the Maoris of New Zealand, the results of their handiwork show a certain dignity and beauty. One forgets that the heads were once those of living men, for they are dehumanized and like sculptures. Each household boasted a few mummies and a number of heads, and, to our surprise, the people willingly showed us their treasures and allowed us to photograph them. In northern Malekula, as we had learned, it is as much as a white man's life is worth to try to see the interior of a head-hut, and demands for heads—or skulls, rather, for the natives of the northern part of the island do not go in for head-curing—are usually met with sullen, resentful silence. Here, the natives not only brought out heads and bodies for us to photograph, but in exchange for a supply of tobacco permitted me to make a flashlight picture of a big ceremonial hut containing about fifty heads and fifteen mummified bodies.

This hut seemed to be a club for the men of the village. Almost every village of the New Hebrides boasts some sort of a club-house, which is strictly taboo for women and children. Here, the devil-devils are made and, it is rumored, certain mysterious rites are performed. Be that as it may, club-life in the New Hebrides seemed to me to be as stupid and meaningless as it usually is in the West. Instead of lounging in plush-covered armchairs and smoking Havana cigars, the men of the New Hebrides lay on the ground and smoked Virginia cuttings in clay pipes. Each man had his favorite resting-place—a hollow worn into the ground by his own body. He was content to lie there for hours on end, almost motionless, saying scarcely a word; but the women and children outside thought that he was engaged in the strange and wonderful rites of his "lodge"!

Toward evening the women of the village appeared with loads of firewood and fruits and vegetables. On top of nearly every load was perched a child or a young baby, its head fitted snugly with a basket to make the skull grow in the way in which, according to Tomman ideals of beauty, it should go. The women of Tomman we found a trifle more independent than those of other islands of the New Hebrides. Of course, their upper front teeth were missing—knocked out by their husbands as part of the marriage ceremony. The gap was the Tomman substitute for a wedding-ring. But on Tomman, as elsewhere in the New Hebrides, wives are slaves. Since a good wife is expensive, costing from twenty to forty pigs, and the supply is limited, most of the available women are cornered by the rich. A young man with little property is lucky if he can afford one wife. He looks forward to the day when he will inherit his father's women. Then he will have perhaps a dozen willing hands to work for him. He will give a great feast and, if he kills enough pigs, he will be made a chief.

When we went back to the ship at sunset, the old man was still doing his solitary dance in front of the devil-devil. In the morning, when we returned to the village, he was already at it, one foot up, one foot down. When we left Tomman, four days after our arrival, he was still going strong. I tried to discover the reason for the performance, but the natives either could not or would not tell me.

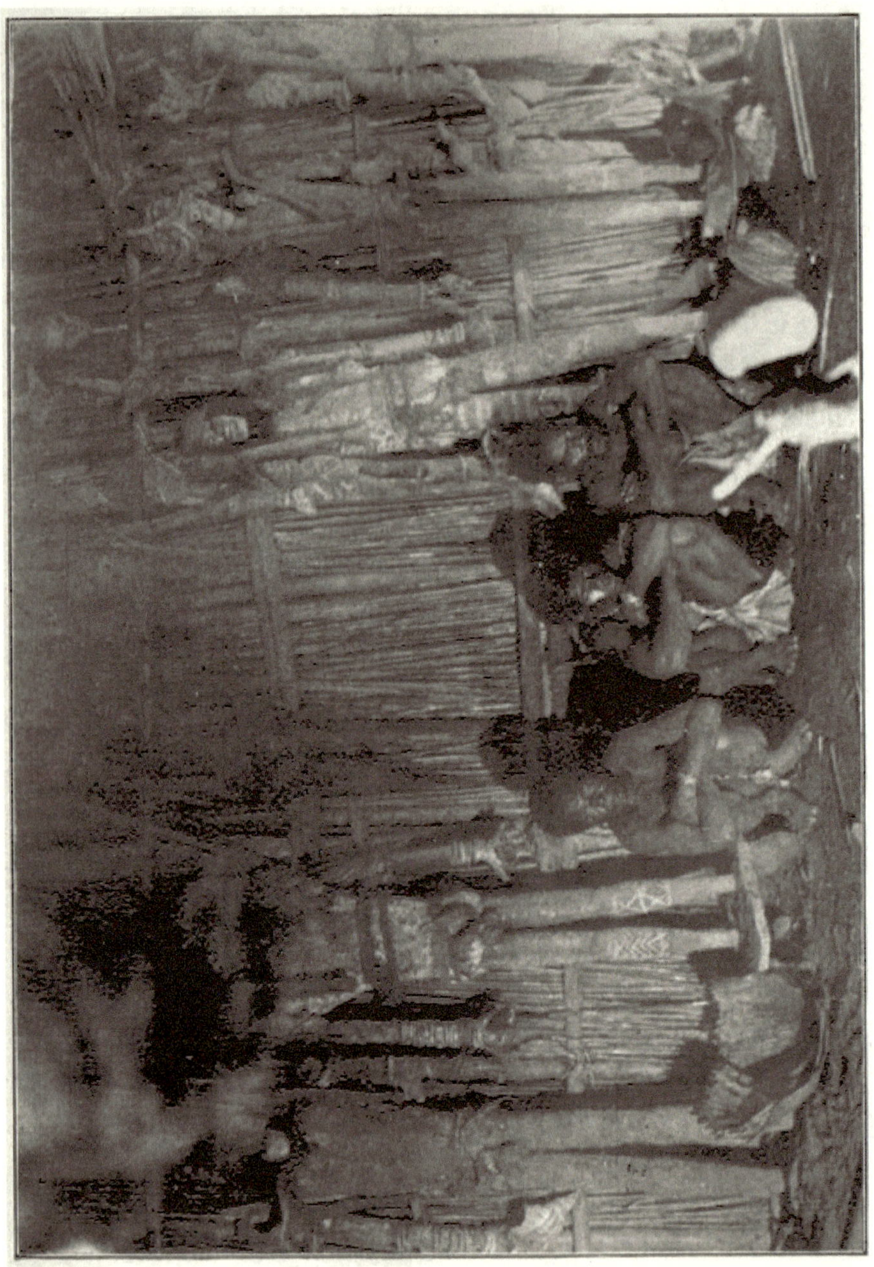

A CLUB-HOUSE IN TOMMAN WITH MUMMIED HEADS AND BODIES

Although Tomman was an interesting spot, we did not remain there long. I was looking for cannibals, and experience had taught me that head-hunters were rarely cannibals or cannibals head-hunters. So, since our time in the islands was growing short, we decided to move on.

CHAPTER XII

THE WHITE MAN IN THE SOUTH SEAS

We chugged away from Tomman and for a week we cruised along the southern end of Malekula. In this region, the mountains come down to the sea. Beyond them lies dangerous territory. It was not safe for us to cross them with the force we had; so we had to be content with inspecting the coast. There we found only deserted villages and a few scattered huts inhabited by old men left to die alone.

Finally we rounded the end of the island and steamed up the eastern coast. One evening we came to anchor in Port Sandwich—a lovely, land-locked bay. Since it was very late, we deferred explorations until the following morning and turned in almost as soon as we had anchored, so as to be ready for work betimes.

At about three o'clock, Osa and I, who slept on deck, were rudely awakened by being thrown into the scuppers. We pulled ourselves to our feet and held tight to the rail. The ship rolled and trembled violently. Though there seemed to be no wind, the water boiled around us and the trees on shore swayed and groaned in the still air.

Captain Moran and his brother came rushing from their cabins. The black crew tumbled out of the hold, yelling with terror. There was a sound of breaking crockery. A big wave washed over the deck and carried overboard everything that was loose. The water bubbled up from below as if from a giant caldron and fishes leaped high into the air. After what seemed to be half an hour, but was in reality a few minutes, the disturbance subsided. We had been through an earthquake.

The volcanic forces that brought the New Hebrides into being are still actively at work. Small shocks are almost a daily occurrence in the islands. But this had been no ordinary earthquake. The next morning, when we went ashore, we found that half the native huts of the little settlement near the mouth of the bay had collapsed like card houses. The devil-devils and boo-boos stood at drunken angles— some of them had fallen to the ground—and, in the village clearings and other level places, the ground looked like a piece of wet paper that had been stretched until it was full of wrinkles and jagged tears. Streaks of red clay marked the courses of landslides down the sides of the mountains. The old men of the settlement said that the earthquake was the worst they had ever experienced. And when we returned to Vao, we found that two sides of our own bungalow had caved in as a result of the shock.

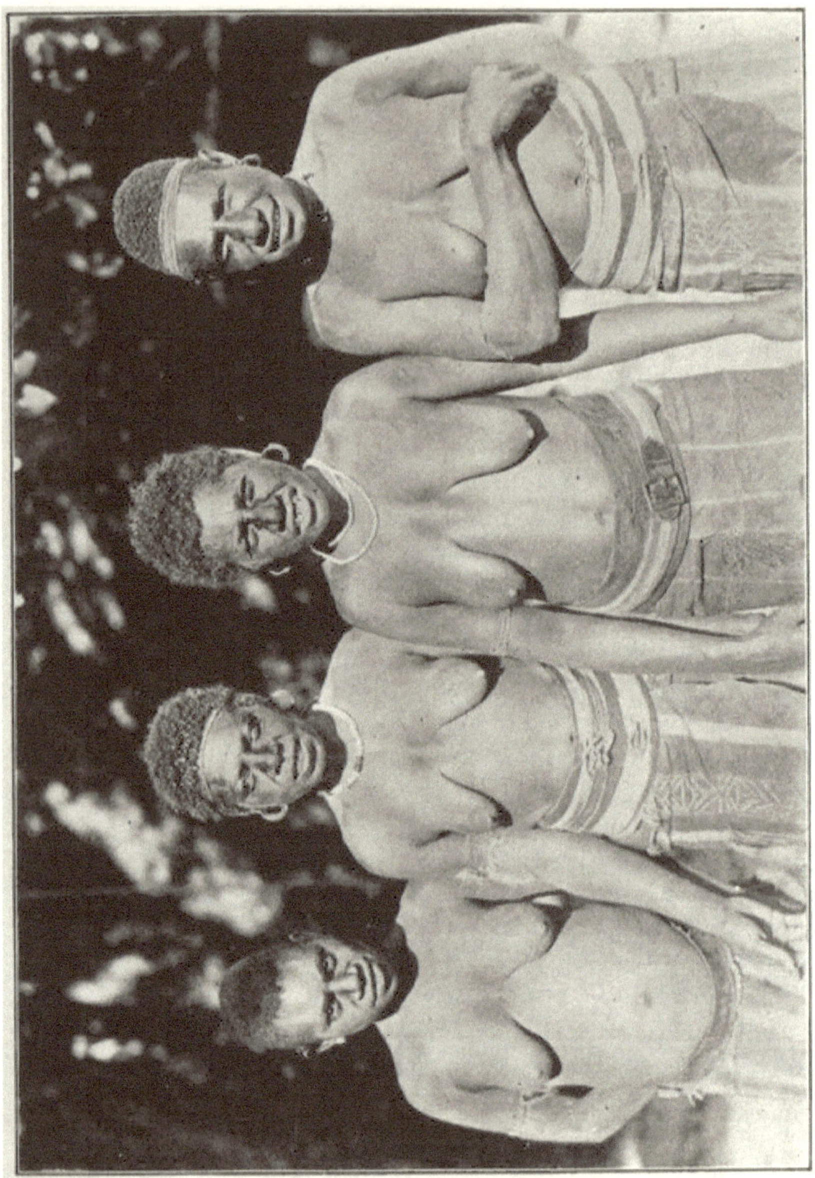

TOMMAN WOMEN, SHOWING GAP IN TEETH

A visit to the volcano Lopevi gave us further proof of the uncertain foundation on which the islands rest.

On the morning after the earthquake, Mr. King, the British Commissioner, appeared in the Euphrosyne, on his way to Vao to fetch us for a visit at Vila. We told him regretfully that we had no time for visiting, and then he proposed a jaunt to Lopevi, a great volcano about thirty miles from Malekula. We were glad of the opportunity to see the volcano, which was reputed to be one of the most beautiful in the world. So we said good-bye to Captain Moran, who departed at once to continue his interrupted trading, and we transferred our belongings to the Euphrosyne, where we reveled in the unaccustomed luxury of good beds and good service by attentive servants.

We left Port Sandwich at daybreak, and in a few hours we saw Lopevi, a perfect cone, rising abruptly out of the water to a height of nearly six thousand feet. When we came within range, I got my camera ready. A fine fringe of thunder-clouds encircled the island about halfway down, but the top was free. The light was perfect. I was grinding happily away, when a miracle happened. Lopevi sent up a cloud of smoke. Then she growled ominously, and shot out great tongues of lapping flame. More smoke, and she subsided into calm again. I had secured a fine picture and congratulated myself on having arrived just in the nick of time. Suddenly, as we discussed the event, Lopevi became active again. And after that there was an eruption every twenty minutes from ten in the morning until four in the afternoon. We steamed all around the island, stopping at favorable points to wait for a good "shot." At four o'clock, we sailed for Api, where we were to harbor for the night. And from the time we turned our backs on Lopevi, there was not another eruption. Her cone was in sight for an hour that night, and next morning, from Ringdove Bay where we were anchored, she was plainly visible. But she did not emit a single whiff of smoke. Osa called her our trained volcano.

We remained on Api for four days. Since Mr. King was due back at Vila, he had to leave on the morning after our arrival; so we took up our quarters with Mr. Mitchell, the English manager of one of the largest coconut plantations on the island.

In more civilized regions one might hesitate before descending, bag and baggage, upon an unknown host, to wait for a very uncertain steamer; but in the islands of the South Seas one is almost always sure of a welcome. The traders and planters lead lonely lives. They have just three things to look forward to—the monthly visit of the Pacifique, a trip once a year to Sydney or New Caledonia, and dinner. For the Englishman in exile, dinner is the greatest event of the day. He rises at daybreak and, after a hasty cup of coffee, goes out on the plantation to see that work is duly under way. He breakfasts at eleven and then sleeps for a couple of hours, through the heat of the day. His day's work is over at six; then he has a bath and a whiskey-and-soda—and dinner. Another drink, a little quiet reading, then off with the dinner clothes and to bed.

Yes, I said dinner clothes. For dinner clothes are as much *de rigueur* in Ringdove Bay as they are on Piccadilly. I, who have a rowdy fondness for free-and-easy dress and am only too glad when I can escape from the world of dinner coats and white ties, suggested, on the second evening of our stay at Api, that, since Mrs. Johnson was used to informal attire, we could dispense, if Mr. Mitchell desired, with the ceremony of dressing.

"But, my dear Johnson," said Mitchell, "I dress for dinner when I am here alone."

That ended the matter. I knew that I was up against an article of the British creed and might as well conform.

When I first went out to the South Seas, I was disposed to regard the punctiliousness in dress of the isolated Britisher as more or less of an affectation. But now I realize that a dinner coat is a symbol. It is a man's declaration to himself and the world that he has a firm grasp on his self-respect. A Frenchman in the islands can go barefooted and half-clothed, can live a life ungoverned by routine, rising at will, going to bed at will, working at will, can throw off every convention, and still maintain his dignity. With the Anglo-Saxon it is different. The Englishman must hold fast to an ordered existence or, in nine cases out of ten, the islands will "get" him.

It is customary to waste a lot of pity on the trader and the planter in remote places—lonely outposts of civilization, but, from my observation, they do not need pity. The man who stays in the islands is fitted for the life there; if he isn't, he doesn't stay, and, if he does stay, he can retire, after fifteen or twenty years, with a tidy fortune.

Of course the road to fortune is a long and hard one. The average planter starts out with a little capital—say five hundred dollars. He purchases a plot of land. The price he pays depends upon the locality in which he buys. In regions where the natives are still fairly unsophisticated, he may get his land for almost nothing. Even where the natives are most astute, he can buy a square mile for what he would pay for an acre back home. His next step is to get his land cleared. To that end, he buys a whaleboat and goes out to recruit natives to act as laborers. He needs five or six blacks. They will build his house and clear his land and plant his coconuts. Since it takes seven years for the coconuts to mature, sweet potatoes and cotton must be planted between the rows of trees. The sweet potatoes, with a little rice, will furnish all the food required by the blacks. The cotton, if the planter is diligent and lucky, will pay current expenses until the coconuts begin bearing.

Though his small capital of five hundred dollars may be eaten up early in the game, the settler need not despair. The big trading companies that do business in the islands will see him through if he shows any signs of being made of the right stuff. They will give him credit for food and supplies and they will provide him with knives, calico, and tobacco, which he can barter with the blacks for the sandalwood and copra that will help balance his account with the companies. And after the first trying seven years, his troubles are about over—if he can get labor enough to keep his plantation going.

Even in the remote islands of the New Hebrides, the labor problem has reared its head. The employer, in civilized regions, has a slight advantage resulting from the fact that men must work to live. In the New Hebrides, indeed all throughout Melanesia, the black man can live very comfortably, according to his own standards, on what nature provides. Only a minimum of effort is required to secure food and clothing and shelter, and most of that effort is put forth by the female slaves he calls his wives. Even the experienced recruiter finds it hard to get the Melanesian to exchange his life of ease for a life of toil. And the inexperienced recruiter finds it very hard. The days when natives could be picked up on any beach are past. The blacks in the more accessible regions know what recruiting means — two years of hard labor, from which there is no escape and from which a man may or may not return home. So the recruiter must look for hands in the interior, where knowledge of the white man and his ways has not penetrated. Even here, the inexperienced recruiter is at a disadvantage. For the experienced recruiter has invariably preceded him.

Each year, the number of available recruits is growing fewer, for the native population is dwindling rapidly. As a result, the cost of labor is high. In the Solomons, one may secure a native for a three years' term at five or six pounds a year in the case of inexperienced workmen, or at nine pounds a year in the case of natives who have already served for three years. In the New Hebrides, planter bids against planter, and the native benefits, receiving from twelve to fifteen pounds a year for his work. The planters complain of the high cost of labor. But the big planters, the capitalists of the South Seas, who have their chains of copra groves, with a white superintendent in charge of each one, certainly do not suffer. I remember being on one big Melanesian plantation on the day when natives were paid for two years' work all in a lump. About four thousand dollars was distributed among the workers. I watched them spend it in the company store. A great simple black, clad in a nose-stick and a yard of calico, would come in and after an hour of happy shopping would go off blissfully with little or no money and a collection of cheap mirrors and beads and other worthless gew-gaws all in a shiny new "bokkus b'long bell." By night, about three thousand dollars had been taken in by the company store-keeper. I was reminded of a rather grimly humorous story of a day's receipts that totaled only $1800 after a $2000 pay-day. When the report reached the main office in Sydney, a curt note was sent to the plantation store-keeper asking what had become of the other $200!

There are certainly two sides to the labor question in the New Hebrides. Yet the whole development of the islands hangs upon cheap and efficient labor. Where it is to come from is a question. The recruiting of Orientals for service in British possessions in the South Seas is forbidden. Even if it were permitted, it would not solve the problem, for the coolie of China or Japan or India is not adapted to the grilling labor of clearing bush.

Mr. Mitchell discussed the labor problem as long and as bitterly as any employer back home. The natives of Api, while friendly and mild, were entirely averse to toil. He had to import hands from other islands. Only occasionally could he persuade the Api people to do a few days' work in order to secure some object "belong white man."

Often they coveted curious things. One morning, during our stay, a delegation of natives appeared and said they had come for "big-fellow-bokkus (box)." A servant, summoned by Mitchell, brought out a wooden coffin, one of the men counted out some money, and the natives shouldered their "bokkus" and went away.

Mitchell laughed as he watched them depart. That coffin had a history. About six weeks previously, a delegation of natives had appeared, with a black who had seen service on a New Zealand plantation acting as spokesman. He informed Mitchell that their old chief was dying and that they had decided to pay him the honor of burying him in "bokkus belong white man." They asked Mitchell if he would provide such a "bokkus" and for how much. Mitchell had a Chinese carpenter and a little supply of timber; so he very gladly consented to have a coffin made. He figured the cost at ten pounds. That appeared to the delegation to be excessive, and they went off to the hills. The next day, however, they reappeared and requested that he make a coffin half the size for half the money. Mitchell protested that a coffin half the size originally figured upon would not be long enough to hold the chief. And they replied that they would cut his arms and legs off to make him fit in. At that, Mitchell, with an eye to labor supply, said that, if they must have a coffin, they must have a proper coffin. He would order the carpenter to make one large enough to hold the chief without mutilation, and he would charge them only five pounds for it, though that meant a loss to him. The carpenter went to work. Most of the village came down to supervise the job, and every few hours, until the coffin was finished, a messenger reported on the chief's condition. When the "bokkus" was at last done, they carried it up the trail with great rejoicing. But the next day they brought it back. The old chief was up and about, and they had no use for it. They laid it down at Mitchell's feet and demanded their money back. Mitchell protested that he had no use for the coffin, either, but they were firm. And he, remembering how difficult it is to get hands in the copra-cutting season, meekly returned the five pounds, and put the coffin in his storehouse. Now, a month later, the old chief had died, and the natives had come for the coffin. We could hear them chanting as they went up the trail.

The next day we set sail on the Pacifique, which had arrived during the night with letters and papers a month old, and we were dropped at Port Sandwich, which was sparsely populated with sullen and subdued savages, to await whatever trader might happen along to take us back to Vao. We had used all our films and were thoroughly tired of Port Sandwich when a trader finally put in an appearance. His boat was a twenty-four-foot launch, barely large enough to contain us and our equipment. When we hoisted our dinghy aboard, its bow and stern protruded several feet beyond the sides of the launch. Next morning, with some misgivings, we set out on the fifty-five-mile journey that would complete our round of Malekula and bring us back to Vao.

We got "home" about four in the afternoon, tired and half-cooked from the broiling sun that had beat down upon us all day. We received a royal welcome. A great crowd of natives met us at the beach, and each seized a box or package and carried it at top speed up to the bungalow. In half an hour everything was in the house. It had been a long time since our Vao neighbors had had any of our tobacco!

CHAPTER XIII

ESPIRITU SANTO AND A CANNIBAL FEAST

For two days we developed films and plates. On the third, we attended what might be called the New Year's celebration of Vao. Fires are made among the islanders by the primitive method by rubbing two sticks together. Though the operation takes only a minute, the savages are too lazy to light a fire every time they need one, so once a year, in the largest house of the village, they make a big fire, which is kept burning to furnish embers from which all the other fires may be lighted. At the end of the year, the fire is put out with great solemnity, and a new one is lighted. The ceremony lasts all day and all night. It is called "killing the Mankki."

On the morning of the festivities, bush natives began to arrive before daylight. The young boys of Vao served as ferrymen. A group of men would come down to the beach at Malekula and shout across the water, and the Vao boys would put out in their funny little crooked canoes—for wood is so scarce that even bent trees are made to do duty as dugouts—and bring back a load of passengers. Natives came from other islands near by. By night, there were more than a thousand people on the islands.

From early in the morning, there was dancing and pig-killing in the clearings of the three villages. The different tribes did not mingle together. One group would come out of the bush into the clearing, dance its dance, kill a score or so of pigs, and then retire into the bush again.

It was bad weather for photography. It rained all day—a fine, drizzling rain. But I worked hard, hoping to secure some good film, for the dances were unusually interesting. One especially good dance was a snake dance, in which the natives brandished small snakes tied to coconut leaves. They are deadly afraid of snakes. They have a saying that holds good pretty much the world over, to the effect that snakes with blunt tails are always poisonous and those with long, pointed tails are harmless. I noted that the snakes used for the dance were very small and of a long-tailed variety. At the end of the dance each man killed his snake and fed it to a pig. Then each man killed a pig.

The slaughter of pigs was enormous. I am sure some five hundred must have been killed during the day—far more than could be eaten. As each pig was killed, his tusks were removed and placed upon platforms that had been erected to hold them. Pigs' tusks are always carefully preserved. They ornament the houses. They form necklaces for the devil-devils. They are placed in the crotches of trees.

I was convinced, as the day wore on, that pork was not the only meat on the bill of fare. It seemed to me that I was at last hot on the trail of cannibalism; the men from Malekula had brought with them strange packages wrapped in leaves, which, I suspected, contained human flesh. The action of the blacks confirmed my suspicion, for they guarded their packages carefully, and would not let me come near with my cameras.

They were threatening in their attitude all day. Even my tobacco did not thaw them out. The Vao people tolerated me, in return for a case of tobacco, but their eyes were far from friendly, and the old men muttered evilly every time they looked our way.

By dark things were getting lively. The mob of savages surged back and forth from one village to another, shouting and singing. I made a great discovery for thirsty America—that people can actually get drunk on imagination. The natives had no intoxicating liquor. Their only drink was water, and yet they lurched drunkenly when they walked, and sang as only drunken men and women sing.

I did not see the fire put out and the new one built. As it grew later, the mob became wilder. I began to think of the long, dark trail to the bungalow, where we would be absolutely at the mercy of lurking savages, and decided that discretion was the better part of valor. So Osa and I went home. We slept with our guns handy—and we did not sleep much at that, for the boo-boos sounded all night and the shouting and singing sometimes surged very near.

We spent the next few days in visits to the northern coast of Malekula, but we did not dare venture inland, for the attitude of the natives was at once suspicious and threatening. We talked the matter over and decided that we had seen about enough of Malekula and Vao and might as well pursue our investigations elsewhere. Espiritu Santo was some forty miles away. In the southern portion there was reported to be a race of dwarfs, and cannibalism was said to be general there, as on Malekula. We had almost despaired of getting actual proof that man ate man in the New Hebrides. We ourselves had seen enough to be convinced that "long pig" was on many a bill of fare, but we could not prove anything; for, since the Government metes out severe punishment to eaters of human flesh, the savages are careful not to be caught at their ghoulish feasts. Still, our luck might turn, we thought, if we changed islands, and we should find the evidence we had been seeking for so many weeks.

The very day after we made this decision, a small cutter nosed into the passage between Vao and Malekula. The owner was a full-blooded Tongan trader, named Powler. He was on his way to get some coconuts he had bought from a native on an island near by, but he promised to return in a few days and take us to Santo. When he arrived, we had our equipment packed and were ready to go aboard. The natives helped us with a will and showed real regret at parting with us, for they knew that they would never again get so much tobacco in return for so little work.

The wind was favorable, and we fairly flew along. Shortly after dark we anchored off Tongoa, a small island a stone's throw from Santo. To my great delight, Powler agreed to remain with us. He was a great, good-natured giant, never out of sorts and strong as an ox. I wished we had met with him sooner. The natives trusted him. His dark skin and his ability to grasp the languages of the island tribes stood him in good stead. Besides, he had the reputation, among both natives and whites, of being absolutely honest in his dealings—a trait as rare in the South Seas as elsewhere. In his company, we went ashore early on the morning after our arrival.

We found the men of Santo, who gathered on the beach to greet us, quite different in type from the Malekula bush savages. They were smaller and more gracefully built. They wore flowers and feathers in their hair. They had a curious custom of removing part of the bone that divides the nostrils so that the bridges of their noses had fallen in and they appeared to be always scowling. To enhance their fierceness still further, they put sticks through their noses.

Such nose ornaments are characteristic of the blacks of the South Seas. The Solomon Islander wears a ring fashioned from bone or shell and highly polished and ornamented. The native of Santa Cruz adorns himself with a piece of polished tortoise-shell shaped like a padlock. But the man of the New Hebrides thrusts into his nose anything that he happens upon—usually a stick picked up along the trail.

To my great delight, the Santo men wore a geestring of calico. As I have said before, the dress of the men of Malekula, if you can call it dress, draws attention to their sex rather than conceals it. On my first visit among them, I had taken motion-pictures of them as they were. When I returned to America, I found that naked savages shocked the public. Some of my best films were absolutely unsalable. On this second trip, accordingly, I managed, whenever possible, to persuade the savages to wear geestrings or loin-cloths or aprons of leaves. Since "costuming" was very difficult (the blacks, naturally enough, could see no reason for it), I was glad that I should not have to spend time in persuading the men of Santo to put on more clothing.

At daybreak on the following morning, we started for the hills. With us were Powler and three of his boys and fifteen trustworthy Tongoa natives. We were bound for a village of pottery-makers—but we never got there. We had tramped for about three hours when we came suddenly upon a group of little men. They were too surprised to run, and too frightened. They were all, with the exception of one of their number who carried a gun as big as he was, armed with bows and arrows, but they did not show any hostility. Instead, they just gathered close together and stared at us in terror.

These were the dwarfs I had heard about. I got out some presents for them. Soon their timidity wore off, and I persuaded them to walk one by one under my outstretched arm. Although their fuzzy wool stood out in great bushy mops, not a hair touched my arm as they passed under. There were sixteen of them, all told. Five were old fellows with grizzled whiskers, ten were of middle age, and one, the tallest of them all, was a boy of about fifteen.

We settled down near a stream and I took pictures as long as the light lasted. That night, our little friends camped close by, and the next day, when we set out for the beach, they followed us. We showed them everything we had in our trunks.

They were as pleased as children, and, when I allowed the old chief to shoot my big automatic revolver, he fairly danced with excitement.

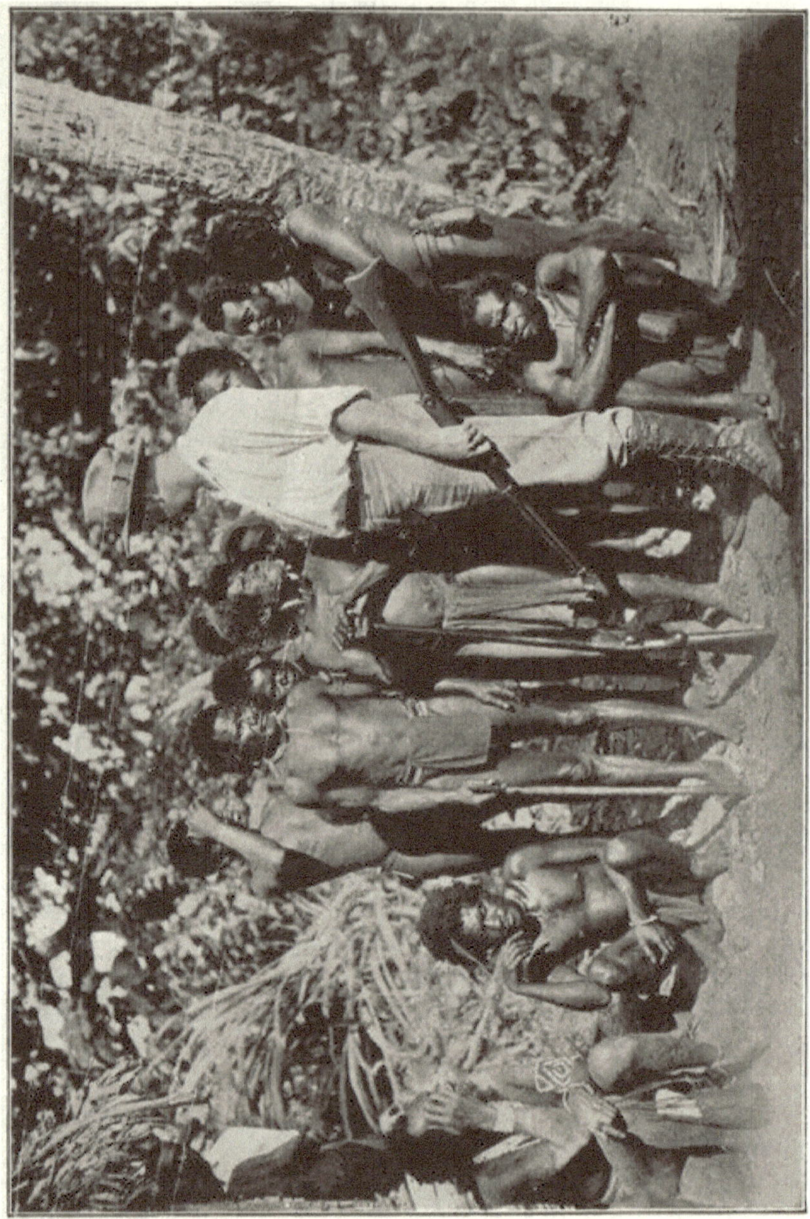

DWARFS OF ESPIRITU SANTO

The next day, I sent messengers into the hills to hunt for a chief about whom Mr. King had told us. This chief had achieved a great reputation as a prophet and a worker of magic. A year before, he had been nobody—just a savage. Then he had gone mad. He had once been recruited as a member of the crew of a mission ship, where he had heard hymns and Bible stories, which he now adapted to his own use. He told the natives there was going to be a great flood, which would cover Santo. He himself, however, would not be drowned, for he was going to bring Hat Island, a little island off the coast, over to rest on Santo Peak. Hat Island was a barren and undesirable piece of real estate, but the prophet said that he had made arrangements to have twenty European steamers come regularly with food and tobacco for the inhabitants. Since he had been fairly successful in foretelling the weather, the natives believed in him, and each clamored for a place on Hat Island. But the salvation offered by the old savage came high. Reservations on Hat Island could be secured only at the price of ten pigs each. Soon the prophet had cornered most of the pigs in that section of Santo. Seeing his power, he raised the price of admission. He secured, in addition to the pigs, the most desirable women in the vicinity. In fact, he appropriated everything he wanted, and occasionally he ran *âmok* and killed several of his compatriots—as he said, to put the fear of God into them.

The next recruiter that came to Santo was besieged with savages begging to be allowed to go to work on copra plantations. He soon learned that the natives had not suddenly grown industrious, but that even work seemed pleasant in contrast with the reign of terror of the inspired chief. The chief saw possibility of profit in the desire of his people to escape and made the recruiter pay heavily in tobacco and calico for every native taken away.

Reports of his rule had reached the Government officers at Vila, and Commissioner King, who had sent for him several times to no avail, had given me a letter to present to the old fellow, in case I should go to Santo. I now sent word to the chief that I had an important message that could be delivered only to him in person. To my surprise, two days after the message had been delivered, the prophet appeared.

I had made everything ready for a motion-picture show to entertain my pigmies. Just before dark, as I was testing my projector, thirty armed natives came down the beach. The dwarfs wanted to run, but we made them understand that we would protect them, and they huddled behind us, frightened, but with perfect faith in our ability and readiness to take care of them in any crisis.

The newcomers were a nasty-looking lot. The prophet, ridiculous in a singlet and overalls and a high hat, came up to me with no sign of hesitation and held out his hand. I could distinguish words in the greeting he grunted at me, but they had no connection. His eyes were bloodshot and wild, his lips were abnormally red, and he drooled as he talked.

I presented Commissioner King's letter, which was an imposing document with a red official seal. In high-sounding language it enjoined the chief to give me and my party every possible aid, and ended with an invitation to his prophetic highness to come to Vila on the Euphrosyne the next time she passed that way and the promise that he would not be harmed if he would do so.

When the prophet saw the red seal, his assurance fell from him, and he rolled his eyes in terror.

"Me sick; me sick," he repeated over and over. I tried to explain that Commissioner King realized that he was sick, and for that very reason wanted to see him and help him, but I doubt if he understood anything I said.

After dark, we started the show. The dwarfs chattered and giggled like children, but our other guests were unsmiling and ominously silent. Only the prophet kept talking. One of the boys told me afterward that he was telling his men that he had sent for me in order to work his magic through me—that I and my projector had nothing to do with the pictures; he himself was responsible.

But halfway through the performance he apparently began to doubt his power. Rocking back and forth, he repeated over and over, "By-em-by me die, by-em-by me die." He was looking forward to the day when he would be captured and carried off to Vila and, as he imagined, put to death. I was glad when the show was over and the prophet and his followers withdrew for the night. It had not been an especially merry evening.

Early next morning a delegation of the prophet's followers sought me out and begged me to take their chief by force to Vila and have him hanged.

"He bad. He takem plenty pigs; he takem plenty women; he killem plenty men," they explained.

I was sorry for them, but I could do nothing. I tried to make them understand that I had nothing to do with the Government and consequently no authority to arrest a man, but I could see that they did not quite believe me. They went off muttering to themselves.

In a few minutes they departed with their chief in quest of a certain kind of shellfish to be found about five miles up the beach, and we decided to take advantage of their absence and visit one of the villages in the prophet's territory.

We walked for about three hours without seeing any signs of a village. Then we heard, faint in the distance, the sound of a tom-tom. Soon we were within hearing of a chanted song. We advanced with caution, until we reached the edge of a village clearing. From behind a clump of bushes we could watch the natives who danced there. The dance was just the ordinary native hay-foot, straw-foot, around the devil-devils in the center of the clearing, now slow, now gradually increasing in tempo until it was a run.

What interested me was the feast that was in preparation. On a long stick, over the fire, were a dozen pieces of meat. More meat was grilling on the embers of another fire. On leaves near by were the entrails of the animal that was cooking. I do not know what it was that made me suspect the nature of this meat. It certainly was not much different in appearance from pork. But some sixth sense whispered to me that it was not pork.

The savages had no suspicion of our nearness. As a matter of fact, the keenness of sight and hearing that primitive peoples are generally credited with are entirely lacking in the New Hebrideans. Many a time Osa and I have quietly crept up to a native village and stolen away again without being detected. Often on the trail we have literally run into blacks before they realized that we were approaching. Even the half-starved native dogs have lost their alertness. More than once I have come suddenly on a cur and laughed at him as he rolled over backward in an attempt to escape. With the natives lost in a dance, we were quite safe.

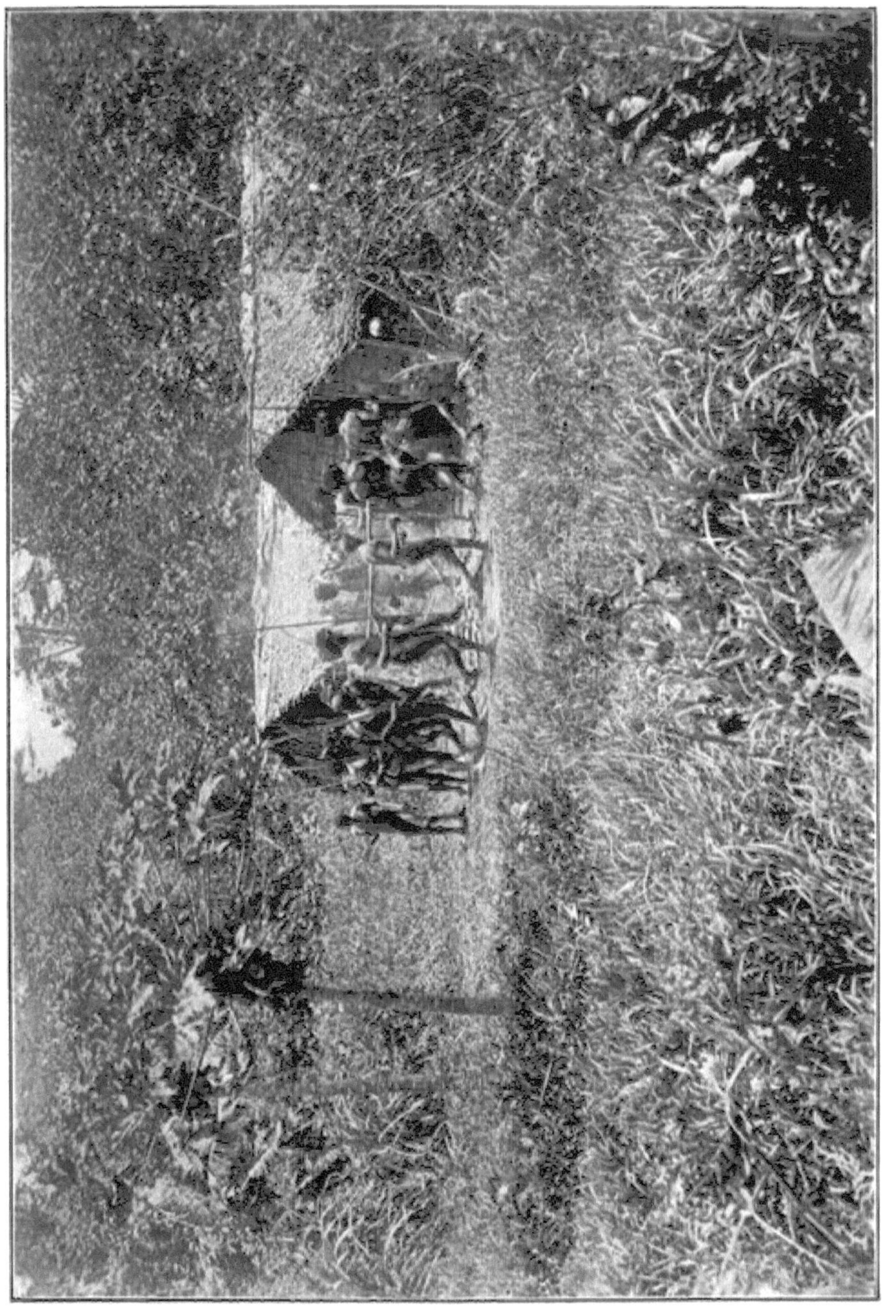

THE CANNIBAL DANCE

For an hour we watched and took long-range photographs. The dance continued monotonously. The meat sizzled slowly over the fire—and nothing happened. Then I gave one of the Tongoa boys who accompanied us a radium flare and told him to go into the clearing, drop the flare into the fire, and run to one side out of the picture. He did as I asked him. The natives stopped dancing and watched him as he approached. He threw the flare into the fire and jumped aside. As they stooped down close to the flame to see what he had thrown there, the flare took fire and sent its blinding white light into their faces. With a yell they sprang back and ran in terror directly toward us. When they saw us, they stopped so quickly that they almost tumbled backward. Then they turned and ran in the opposite direction. The half-minute flare had burned out; so they grabbed the meat from the fire and carried it with them into the bush.

My boys sprang into the clearing. I, with my camera on my shoulder, was just behind them. When I came up to them, they were standing by the fire, looking at the only remnant of the feast that was left on the embers. It was a charred human head, with rolled leaves plugging the eye-sockets.

I had proved what I had set out to prove—that cannibalism is still practiced in the South Seas. I was so happy that I yelled. After photographing the evidence, I wrapped the head carefully in leaves, to take away with me. We picked the fire over, but could find no other remainder of the gruesome feast. In one of the huts, however, we discovered a quantity of human hair, laid out on a green leaf, to be made into ornaments.

Some of the cannibals returned and, from a distance, watched us search their huts. I then took their pictures. They grinned into the camera, as innocent as children.

We arrived at the beach a little after dark. Powler had shot some pigeons, fried their breasts, and made a soup from the remainder, and he had cut down a coconut tree and made a salad of the heart. We did full justice to the meal. After it was over, we sat and admired the roasted head—at least I admired it. Osa did not think much of it. As for Powler, he tried in vain to conceal that he thought me absolutely crazy to care so much about an old charred head.

The next day, while I was printing pictures on the beach, a delegation of cannibals appeared on the scene. They were good-natured and friendly. I showed them a big mirror. It was apparently the first they had ever seen. They were awed and puzzled, touching the glass with cautious fingers and looking behind the mirror suddenly, to surprise whoever might be fooling them. I photographed them as they peered at their reflection and grimaced like a bunch of monkeys. We invited them to luncheon. Their favorite dish of "long pig" was not on the bill of fare. But they ate our trade salmon and biscuits with gusto and smacked their lips over the coffee that Osa made for them—the first they had ever tasted. They remained with us until the following day, when we picked up our apparatus and sailed off on the first lap of our journey home.

In seven months in the New Hebrides I had exposed twenty-five thousand feet of film, and had, besides, about a thousand "stills." I was well satisfied with my work; for I knew that my pictures would help the Western world to realize the life lived by the fast-disappearing primitive races of the earth; and I had actual evidence—my long-range photographs and the charred head that I so carefully cherished—that cannibalism is still practiced in the islands of the South Seas.

THE END

Lector House believes that a society develops through a two-fold approach of continuous learning and adaptation, which is derived from the study of classic literary works spread across the historic timeline of literature records. Therefore, we aim at reviving, repairing and redeveloping all those inaccessible or damaged but historically as well as culturally important literature across subjects so that the future generations may have an opportunity to study and learn from past works to embark upon a journey of creating a better future.

This book is a result of an effort made by Lector House towards making a contribution to the preservation and repair of original ancient works which might hold historical significance to the approach of continuous learning across subjects.

HAPPY READING & LEARNING!

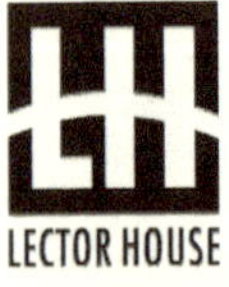

LECTOR HOUSE LLP
E-MAIL: lectorpublishing@gmail.com